The
Grace
to
Race

The Wisdom and Inspiration of the
80-Year-Old World Champion Triathlete
Known as the Iron Nun

SISTER MADONNA BUDER
with Karin Evans

Simon & Schuster
New York   London   Toronto   Sydney

Simon & Schuster
1230 Avenue of the Americas
New York, NY 10020

First Simon & Schuster hardcover edition October 2010

SIMON & SCHUSTER and colophon are registered trademarks of Simon & Schuster, Inc.

For information about special discounts for bulk purchases, please contact Simon & Schuster Special Sales at 1-866-506-1949 or business@simonandschuster.com.

The Simon & Schuster Speakers Bureau can bring authors to your live event. For more information or to book an event, contact the Simon & Schuster Speakers Bureau at 1-866-248-3049 or visit our website at www.simonspeakers.com.

Designed by Jill Putorti

Manufactured in the United States of America

10   9   8   7   6   5   4   3   2   1

Library of Congress Cataloging-in-Publication Data

Buder, Madonna, Sister
    The grace to race : the wisdom and inspiration of the 80-year-old world champion triathlete known as the iron nun / Sister Madonna Buder with Karin Evans.
        p.   cm.
    1. Buder, Madonna, Sister.   2. Athletes—United States—Biography.
3. Nuns—United States—Biography.   4. Athletes—Religious life.
5. Triathlon.   6. Ironman triathlons.   I. Evans, Karin.   II. Title.
    GV697.B84A3   2010
    796.092—dc22
    [B]   2010022660

ISBN 978-1-4391-7748-8
ISBN 978-1-4391-7750-1 (ebook)

To my Creator, the Gift-Giver,
and to my devoted parents

Contents

Introduction

THE FIRST TIME I ever heard about Sister Madonna Buder she had been blown off her bicycle, landing head first on the Queen Ka'ahumanu Highway. She was competing in the 2000 Hawaiian Ironman, speeding downhill on the Big Island. Hunched over her handle bars, the Hawaiian sun beating down on her back, she was caught off guard by a strong side gust. Suddenly she was airborne, her bike and body carried two yards before being deposited on the lava road. She suffered a fractured jaw and broken collarbone, plus it took a dozen stitches to close up the damage to her face.

When I reached her by phone just two weeks later and gingerly asked her how she was doing, almost the first words out of her mouth were, "I just can't wait to get back on that bicycle!" It had taken forty-five minutes for the ambulance to arrive that day. While she lay there waiting, she felt no fear, no despair. "I was going lickety-split," she recounted. "I can't really explain it, but I felt comfortable lying there in my wreckage. I just thought, How can I pull out of this?"

Her strongest feeling was a swelling of gratitude for two of her fellow competitors, a man and a woman who jumped off their bicycles and came to her aid. "That was the real miracle," she said. "They didn't even get to finish their own race."

What the pair who stayed by her side found most remarkable was this: The racer lying in the road, who until that moment had been competing in one of the most grueling athletic events on earth, was not only a Roman Catholic nun—she was seventy years old.

For most people of whatever age, that crash might have ended their competitive days. For Sister Madonna, it was just a brief interruption. "If I'd been airborne any higher, I'd be flapping my wings!" she exclaimed to me in her lovely, lyrical voice. At this remark she actually giggled, then added, "I lay there in a pool of my own blood and thought, Well, Lord, I'm not going to finish this race today but I'm going to be all right. I just remember feeling at peace."

When Sister Madonna laced up a pair of hand-me-down sneakers to take a run down the beach at age forty-eight, no one could have predicted that someday she'd be a world champion, eventually known as the Iron Nun, the Running Nun, the Mother Superior of Triathlon. Yet four years later, after she tackled the Boston Marathon at the age of fifty-two, the writer and famous runner George Sheehan noted with admiration, "God was watching Sister Madonna Buder and she knew it."

Today, after thirty-one years of competition, Sister Madonna holds dozens of records, including International Triathlon Union World Championships, as well as age group records for the Hawaiian and Canadian Ironman events—each of which requires a 2.4–mile swim, a 112–mile bicycle ride, and a full marathon of 26.2 miles. In 1999, she was honored by the USA Triathlon Organization and *Competitor* magazine as the female Grandmaster Triathlete of the Year. Two years later, she was given the Iron Spirit Award by the International Triathlon Union World Championship committee.

Her records in some cases apply not just to her own age group, but to younger categories as well. In fact, she routinely has outpaced both men and women who are far younger than she is. In one race, as Sister Madonna sailed by a group of sixty-year-olds, no one was too surprised. Then she passed some fifty-year-olds, and began gaining on the forties. A cheer went up from the younger crowd. "Do you believe it?" "Way to go!" "I hope I look that good when I am seventy!" She's managed to outrun—literally—two of her physicians, themselves triathletes and younger than she is, who have helped her through various exercise-induced traumas.

At competitive events, Sister Madonna is sought out for her inspiring presence and her spiritual advice. Often, before a race, she can be found huddled with other runners, praying for them and with them. Race directors often ask her to bless the crowd before the race begins—or maybe put in a good word for decent weather. "She spreads the message of positive spirit, inspiration, and love to a lot of people," says a race organizer.

As the years have passed, Sister Madonna has gone on to finish events that most people her age wouldn't think of trying. In 2005, the age 75–79 category was created for her at the Hawaiian Ironman in Kona, where she set the record as the oldest woman ever to finish. She did this just eight weeks after she suffered a broken elbow in a bicycle crash during a qualifying race.

She runs with a steel plate in one hip and metal screws and pins in both elbows—her "scrap metal," she calls it. "No wonder I am an 'iron woman.' My right arm has suffered six incidents. It's a wonder it's still hanging on." In 1987, she ran the last eight miles of the Hawaiian Ironman with a fractured right foot. In 1988, she competed with two broken toes; and in 2000, there was that horrific bicycle crash in Hawaii.

"I do it by putting one foot in front of the other," she says, "although there have been some dark moments out there."

In 2008, at the age of seventy-eight, the Iron Nun ran the Boston Marathon again, twenty-five years after her debut. That year she also competed in more than a dozen triathlons and fifteen Senior Olympics events. In some instances, she actually improved on her former times. When a Canadian gerontologist asked her about this achievement, she simply said, "Well, that's what's fun about this. You know, after a certain number of years, you're competing with yourself, because if you live long enough, everybody else falls by the wayside. So you either have to choose men to beat because there are no women, or beat up on yourself."

At least one physician has expressed interest in studying Sister Madonna to learn what gives her the physical edge she seems to have. But Sister Madonna has resisted submitting herself to such studies. She'd rather be out doing good works or running through the woods than spinning her wheels on a treadmill, hooked up to wires.

You couldn't meet a better argument for exercise—extreme exercise. Sister Madonna's eyes are a lovely blue, her skin is radiant, her hair is still medium brown with a few wisps of blonde, and if you look closely, some gray. She's willowy and strong—5 feet 7 inches tall, 115 pounds, 7 percent body fat, with the grit of a rugby player and the grace of a dancer. It is a little hard not to envy her energy, her infectious joy, her long, tanned legs.

She travels from event to event on a wing and a prayer—asking for rides, camping out, sleeping in her car if necessary. She trusts she'll get where she's going, with some heavenly help and a few angels along the way. God, she says, is her travel agent.

As she neared her eightieth birthday, Sister Madonna set a goal to return to Kona in 2010 to open up yet another age division for women—80 to 84—and to be yet again the oldest woman to finish the Hawaiian Ironman. "There is this interior voice, or seventh sense, to which I try to be attentive," she says. "I am always running in God's presence, admiring His Creation. There is something urging me on."

—*Karin Evans*

I

The Miracle Finish—
2006 Hawaiian Ironman

*Determination is the mind willing something to happen
by the grace of God.*

Kona, Hawaii
October, 2006

I WAS A fourth of the way through the 2.4-mile swim course of
the Hawaiian Ironman, wondering why I didn't seem to be making any progress through the water. I raised my head, peering
through my goggles at a landmark hotel on shore, and realized
I wasn't getting beyond it. I kept stroking, wondering what was
going on in the ocean depths below. When I finally reached land,
it was twenty minutes later than I had expected.

In the transition area between the swim and the bike course,
I peeled off my damp suit as quickly as I could. Every second
counts in these races. When I got on my bicycle, it wasn't long
before I realized it didn't matter if I had just gotten out of the
ocean. The rain was coming down so heavily that I had to close
my eyes every few seconds. This called for extra precaution,
which slowed me down considerably.

Ironman events, with their swim-bike-run requirement—
140.6 miles in all, with a full marathon at the end—are grueling
enough without this sort of weather. But there was no question
of giving in to it, although it might be normal to wonder what I
was doing out here at the age of seventy-six.

Aside from the usual competitiveness involved in this famed
annual event on the Big Island of Hawaii, I had my own special
reason for wanting to finish. My nephew Dolph had died the
previous month, quite unexpectedly. (It wasn't until six months
later that the coroner's report said the cause was heart disease.)
So I had been asking God for some kind of confirmation that
he had died at peace and was in the right place. I made a kind
of deal with God: If I could finish this race, I would know my
nephew was at peace. That thought was in the back of my mind
as I struggled through the ocean swim, and it was on my mind
now, as I did my best to keep pedaling through the torrents of
rain.

By the time I got to the transition between the bike segment
and the run, I was beginning to feel a little queasy, something
that has happened to me on the run for the past ten years or so.
My stomach doesn't always cooperate with the rest of my body,
and that condition forces me to walk almost the entire marathon.

This time, after spending twenty-eight minutes in the bike-
to-run transition, trying to get some nourishment down and get
reconditioned for my death march, I managed to start out on
the run, but had gone only about five of the 26.2 miles when a
marshal on a moped came alongside me and began spitting out
statistics: "You are three minutes down." I was still trying to run,
but thinking, "What is he telling me? Maybe he means I am
three minutes from making the cutoff time. Guess I had better

pick up the pace, whether or not I feel like it." The Ironman rules require that you make the three disciplines of swim, bike, and run within a given time. The next time he encountered me, he prompted, "You're doing better. You are up three minutes."

Three miles later came the deluge. It was coming down the mountain slopes and across the road in a river ankle-deep. I had on my lightest running shoes, yet I could barely lift my feet. Afraid the current was going to knock me down in my weakened state, I got the inspiration to cross over to the other side of the road, moving on a diagonal toward the sidewalk. As I stepped on the submerged curb, my foot slipped, which sent me sprawling. I didn't even take time to see if I was gushing blood, figuring the rain would take care of that. It looked as if everyone, even the marshal, had headed for dry cover. However, this couple appeared suddenly from nowhere and yanked me to my feet.

It had gotten cooler, and I was sopping wet and beginning to feel chilled. Being vulnerable to hypothermia, I prayed, "Lord, let me just keep moving, no matter how. At least I will be circulating." I promised myself that by mile 15 I would try some hot chicken soup at the aid station there. Meanwhile, the marshal on the moped putt-putted up again, announcing that I was now eight minutes down. Nonetheless I kept plodding. As long as I was ambulatory the thought of quitting was not an option.

When I did get to the aid station at mile 15, I stopped and accepted some chicken soup, which was lukewarm, probably from rain water. It did not settle well, so I grabbed a piece of soft roll, hoping it would sop up the remains in my gurgling stomach. One bite—and that came up too. As I sat exhausted in the aid station, one of the volunteers started massaging my shoulders. I did not want to leave. Then came the inner command: "You had better get up now. No one is going to finish this race for you." It was late, and though I wanted to linger, I had to get going.

I got back on my feet and struggled onwards in the darkness, toward the turnaround. With about six miles to go, I was out there alone when these four angels appeared from the opposite side of the road, running in the dark. One had no shoes. One had only thongs. A husband-and-wife team were the only two with running shoes. Imagine my surprise when one of them asked, "May we accompany you in?"

At this point, I was only walking, and murmured weakly, "Uh-huh." Then they asked whether I would like them to tell me a story as we moved along, or if I wanted to tell them one. "You," I said. The couple began telling me about their young daughter, who had broken her arm. After occupying me with the details of how she had bravely overcome her injury and how proud they were of her, they changed the subject. "Do you see that stop sign ahead? Do you think you can start running when you get there, and then stop at the next signal to walk again?" They kept pushing me on in this manner.

The next time the marshal on the moped appeared and started spitting out statistics, I completely blocked him out, figuring my angels would interpret the timing for me. I don't wear a watch during these events. Even if I did, I wouldn't be able to see it in the darkness. I just listen to my body. After all, that is the most accurate measurement. When your battery runs low, you just can't go.

Then along came another person on a moped, a man I'd known a long time as an announcer for many triathlon events. I found out later that he, too, had come on the scene to encourage me, and was radioing ahead to the finish line. "It doesn't look as if Sister Madonna is going to make it. She is just walking now." And then a bit later: "Oh, she just passed another runner, so maybe there is hope." He kept the reports flowing so as to hype up everyone at the finish line to keep up their prayers. Even the local Hawaiian fire dancers were going through their ceremonial rituals on my behalf.

I was, of course, totally unaware of any of this. Meanwhile, I begged my angels, "Can't I just walk until we get to Palani Hill, and then I'll start running down it a mile and a half from the finish? Since we'll be back in civilization, it won't matter if I collapse."

They were firm. "No, you have to do a bit more running before you get there." With a mile and two-tenths to go, someone noticed I had only twelve minutes left if I was going to make it to the finish in time. That did not seem possible. All I knew was to rely on the advice of my remaining two angel coaches. The other two, running without shoes, could no longer keep pace and had peeled off, but the pair still with me kept telling me when I should run and when I could walk.

My little twosome team kept encouraging me onward. Closer to the finish line, I could hear the crowd in a frenzy. When we got to the top of the final hill, I started extending my legs for a downhill run. They yelled a last admonition, "Oh, good, don't stop! Keep going, even when you get to the bottom of the hill!"

From the outset, as I had begun preparing for this 2006 Hawaiian Ironman, there had been strange omens, beginning with my nephew Dolph's death just the month before. Before I left home in Spokane, I had the gut feeling that this was going to be a very different competition. I'd done the Hawaiian Ironman some twenty times by now, but something this year felt different. The feeling I had didn't tell me not to go; it just said, be prepared.

On my way to Hawaii, I drove from my home in Spokane over to Seattle, where I was going to spend the night with friends before boarding for Kona the next day. In Seattle, my friend opened the door, saying, "Do you know what happened in Hawaii?" She turned on the TV, and there was news of an earthquake. That never happens there, I thought. They are used to hurricanes in Hawaii, but not earthquakes. I remembered that premonition.

While watching the news, I wasn't sure whether I could take the plane I was scheduled to take the next day. Flights were turning back because Honolulu was affected and there were power outages. I got on the Web site for the Ironman and learned that, as far as they could see, the course had not been damaged except in one place, and that was under repair. So I decided to go. But for some reason, this little voice said, "Don't go through Honolulu this year to change planes; go through Maui." And so I rebooked my flight through Maui.

As my plane from Seattle neared the islands, it did not look like the Hawaii I knew. Heavy clouds had darkened the usually azure waters. When we touched down on the airstrip, there was water everywhere. It had not stopped raining all day. The plane was late, and we had to run for our connection. None of our checked luggage, including our bicycles, made it to Kona on the flight, and it was not until the next day that they were delivered. But in Honolulu, I heard, passengers hadn't even been able to get off their planes because of power outages.

Grateful to have arrived safely in Kona, I settled into bed.

About half past midnight, I was awakened by this funny rumbling sound. As dishes danced in the cupboard and the bedstead jitterbugged, I thought, "Oh, Lord, you are not finished yet!" At 5:38 a.m. there was another bed-shaker, and I thought, "Are we going to have this race or not? There are only four days left. Please get it out of your system."

It was overcast and cooler than normal on race day, and I thought, Lord this is good—as long as you keep it overcast, there will be minimal winds and no one blown off their bikes.

Then the skies opened.

My angels' last instructions—"Don't stop, even when you get to the bottom of the hill!"—kept ringing in my ears. How did they know I always stopped at the bottom to walk the next five miserable blocks on the flat until I hit Alii Drive and then gave it my all to the finishing chute? Even without a wristwatch, I sensed this was going to be a fight against time. It was then I realized this was the opportunity I had been looking for. If I could cross the finish line in time, I would know that my nephew was at peace and in the right place.

As soon as I made that bargain with God, I had the strangest feeling, as if I were dangling between two realities, losing touch with my body and being conscious only of my momentum. I sensed a presence in the dark over my right shoulder, intimating that what I was doing was unreal. It was like make-believe. When people started crowding in, I heard their yelling and saw their hands outstretched for a high five, but I didn't acknowledge them, which I usually would do. This time, a word of warning came: "If you touch just one of them, it could alter your forward movement. In your weakened condition, it could cost you seconds, which you can't spare." I developed tunnel vision, looked straight ahead and kept pushing.

Usually the Hawaiian Ironman marathon finishes under an arch, but now I saw that they had built a plank that required you to run uphill. How sadistic could it get? But I gave it my all in a last surge. "Oh God, please keep this body moving!" When I topped the finish, the crowd was wild, as well as the announcer. The woman I had stayed with in Kona put a lei over my head, and I immediately bent over with the dry heaves.

When I finally straightened up, I saw projected on the screen my time of 16 hours, 59 minutes, and 3 seconds. I was the last official finisher, the oldest woman on the course, and I had beat the cut-off time of 17 hours by a mere 57 seconds. "Thank you, Lord," I breathed. "Now I know my nephew is in the right place."

When the announcer thrust the microphone in my face, I told him how I had asked God to let me know that my nephew was at peace. Even the announcer danced up and down shouting, "Yeah, he's in the right place! He's in the right place!"

This will forever remain the most significant Ironman I have ever done.

During the awards ceremony the following evening, an announcer on stage was saying something about a Spirit of Determination award. The master of ceremonies kept rattling on about this person going through so many accidents but still coming back for more to compete year after year. I thought that sounded somewhat familiar, but knew it could also apply to lots of other people who train for these events. When I glanced up at the screen on the stage, however, under the words *Spirit of Determination* was my name.

I was seated far back, so it took me a while to gallop through the crowds and up to the staging platform, where I spotted this new Cannondale bike. I could scarcely believe this was my reward, even when the announcer said, "This is yours." Who on earth would think of getting an award like this for being the last official finisher in an event? The bike delivered to me in Spokane several months later was a beautiful heavenly blue.

This was in October. At Thanksgiving when I spoke on the phone with my nephew's family, I shared the details of this event, including the surprise of the Cannondale bike. You could hear a pin drop on the other end of the line. Finally my niece said, "I don't usually pay attention to brand names, but what did you say that bike was?" When I repeated the description she blurted, "That's it! That was the make!" Dolph, she said, had always ridden a Cannondale. What further confirmation did I need that he was in the right place?

In Kona just the year before, I had opened up a new age group for women, 75–79. Now, in 2006, while on stage accepting my award, I promised the crowd that in 2010 I would try to open up yet another age group for women, 80–84. So far, no woman over the age of eighty had attempted an Ironman, though one eighty-year-old man had finally succeeded. If Robert McKeague could do it for the men, I owed it to the women to do likewise.

Sometimes I ask myself about continuing to compete in these Ironman events, but my body, mind, and soul feel so complete while I'm out there. I didn't begin running until I was forty-eight years old, but exercise has redirected my life.

* * *

After the miraculous finish in the 2006 Kona Ironman, I continued to be struck by the integrity of those four people who picked me up the last six miles to encourage me into the finish. I wanted to find out who they were. I learned they belonged to the Oakley Team, obtained their names, and wanted to thank them, so I e-mailed the following:

Dear Brent and Susie,

I want to thank you for being my "angel coaches" during the last portion of the marathon in Kona. Whatever put it in your hearts to do such a thing? Exactly when did you peel off? Did you hear me at the finish line? How did you ever know to tell me not to stop running at the bottom of the hill? I always do! Your manner of coaching me into running was superb, but how could you have timed it so well? After seeing the coverage of this event, I am still in awe of what you did for me. What selflessness!

Would you please thank the other two "angels" who peeled off sooner than the two of you did and pass this message along? Which one was barefooted and which had the thongs? Of course I'd like the answer to the above questions if you feel so inclined, but no rush.

Here's their reply:

Dear Sister Madonna,

How sweet of you to get in touch with us. We should thank you for making the Ironman experience so memorable for us. YOU did all the work and we just had fun. Congratulations!

To answer your questions, as far as I understand, it had become somewhat of a tradition for these sales guys from Oakley, my husband Brent included, to go out on the course about 10:30 p.m. and run in with anyone who might want or need some motivation at the end. They have made this an annual tradition as they are there every year for the event.

The guys on the motor bikes were helping us to pace you, but I myself could hardly believe that it was so close! We peeled off right before you finished, and yes, we did hear you at the finish line. You did all the work, we were just there for support. Actually, my husband Brent had [joined the race to run at your side] with you a few years back, although it wasn't quite as close [a finish] back then. He remembers that you mentioned you wanted to run down the hill and then take a rest, but the wonderful Ironman official on the scooter gave us the sign that there was no time, so we just did our best to keep you going. And, wow! Did you keep going!

Kona Ironman has become a very special event to us, as it is one of the few places where you can see people all coming together to challenge themselves, cheer, volunteer, and show kindness to one another all in one place at one time. It definitely restores some faith that there is some goodness left in the world. We are so happy to have heard from you. Thank you for being such a great motivation to us.

Brent and Susie Lantz

Running does change people's lives. When I first entered the religious life at the age of twenty-three, I was set apart from the world. Once I began to run and to compete, my path opened wide to include the whole world. God's ways are not our ways. I would probably be less effective sitting in the convent than I am now, being thrust into the public where I can influence people by example.

I'm keenly aware how blessed I am, because how many people get angels helping them along the way like I do? I travel alone all the time, and I train alone all the time; but somebody is always there when I need them if something goes wrong.

When people come up to me, as they continually do, and say, "Well, you have an added advantage. God is on your side," I know that it isn't just my advantage. We all have it if we just call on the God power within. It's there for the taking.

2

In the Beginning

Living is the adventure of a lifetime!

Saint Louis, Missouri
July, 1930

I WAS BORN during a July heat wave in Saint Louis, Missouri. It was 105 degrees. Maybe that accounts for the fact that I can withstand high temperatures so well today. I love the sun.

My inherited athletic abilities come from my father, Gustavus A. Buder, Jr., who was a champion oarsman in his younger days. My mother was an oarsman's widow until the Century Boathouse on the Mississippi River in Saint Louis burned down. My father worked as an attorney but carried on the family tradition of philanthropy. The Buder name is emblazoned on many Saint Louis edifices—county library, school, park, office building, and student center on the Maryville University campus—because of my father and his father. My mother, Kathryn M. Buder, founded the Washington University Center for Indian Studies. My grandfather, G. A. Buder, Sr., was one of the founders of the

Saint Louis Municipal Opera and built Saint Louis's landmark Buder Building near the riverfront. My father went to his office there every day until he was eighty-three. Near the end of my father's life the Buder Building's future had been in litigation for two years. The historical society wanted to preserve it, but lost the battle to developers. Forty days after the elegant old building was demolished, my father let go of life. It was a shock to his system to watch it being imploded.

My early life was blessed. I was always outdoors and became an accomplished equestrian. My life was filled with adventures and near misses: capsized sailboats, sledding mishaps, mountaineering ordeals, crashes on roller skates. But somehow I survived it all.

Both of my parents were only children, and had limited experience with the opposite sex. My mother was attracted to my father as a prince who rescued her from her predictable life and opened up a life of adventure. She loved the stage as a young woman, and her beauty and dramatic roles in local theatrical productions captivated my father—especially when he discovered that the role of Shylock in *The Merchant of Venice* could be convincingly portrayed by a woman. He sought to be introduced to her, which my grandmother willingly did. This budding romance interrupted what could have developed into a full-scale acting career, as my mother's drama teacher at the Morse School of Expression was preparing her for Broadway. Since my mother had led a sheltered childhood, her mother was hardly in favor of her leaving the city of Saint Louis for the Big Apple, so she encouraged the relationship. Daddy was in law school at the time. After their engagement, he insisted that they wait to marry until he graduated from Washington University in Saint Louis with his law degree, which he did at age twenty-eight when she, in turn, was a legal twenty-one.

And what opposites they were! He was a conscientious young lawyer and a Unitarian. He was the product of a staunch German upbringing and was set in his ways—systematic, analytical, and practical. Her family came from France, she was born and raised a Catholic, and embraced her faith. Being an only child whose father abandoned her at birth, she was overprotected and not allowed to mingle with playmates. She developed a rich fantasy life, playing with dolls, dressing them, and making up stories as a way to escape the boredom of pent-up apartment living.

What kept my parents together all those years? Did they simply balance each other's opposite qualities, or were they bonded through some sort of heroic effort? Whatever the reason, their long marriage was a source of inspiration to many who knew them through their golden anniversary and beyond.

I too have felt the blessing of this union, this blending and balancing of opposites. At times, though, I have felt within me an inner tension as one or the other of their qualities strives for ascendancy. Eventually, though, I have found the creative, artistic, spiritual, and idealistic side of my mother's French origins merging nicely with the adventurous, realistic, and practical outlook of my father's German tradition. A combination of these two characteristics has served me well throughout my life both as a nun and triathlete.

My father played handball until he was seventy. After his eightieth birthday, he not only continued going to his office six days a week, but came home to put in an intense three to seven hours of weekend gardening—setting a pace for the pacemaker that had been installed when he was sixty-eight.

My mother continued to perform in plays, care for her roses, study French, paint, and write.

When I came along, their first child, I was not the hoped-for gender. My father's father, bless him, had been pressuring my mother to deliver a boy, so that the Buder family name might be perpetuated. My mother, though sorry not to oblige, was grateful that I was healthy, and secretly enjoyed the fact that I was a girl. Shortly after my birth, my paternal grandmother died and left my grandfather in such a severe state of mourning that he eventually became bedridden. His doctors did not know what to do for him.

Since my grandfather would not come to our house to visit me, my parents decided to take me to him when I was about eight months old. He scarcely opened his eyes to look at us, so they placed me on his stomach. I must have been attracted to his bewhiskered face, because I wiggled up his chest and reached out my little hand to touch it. This was all it took. From then on, I was his "little queen," and it no longer concerned him that I wouldn't be carrying on the family name, especially since another baby was soon on the way.

My grandfather lived for another twenty-four years, and the two of us became constant companions. One Sunday morning, my parents awoke to find my crib empty. They looked everywhere, and just as they were ready to call the police, they heard the front door open. In walked my grandfather with a bundle in his arms. In his loneliness, he had come during his sleepless hours to fetch me for a Sunday drive. My parents had words with him, but it didn't break his habit. The two of us went on to have many outings. When the family namesake did arrive thirteen months later, my position had been firmly established. I would sit in my grandfather's lap, and he would tell me tall tales. On Sundays, we would all drive to Grandfather's house for brunch. Sometimes my grandfather and I would play that we were on a steamship and spit cherry pits over the imaginary side rail to see whose would go the farthest. He'd hang the double cherries over my ears like earrings. As I grew older, he taught me to play cards and taught me about the practicalities of math through thought problems.

Even in the cradle, I was a baby on the go. In one of my father's home movies of me as an infant, I appear to be doing push-ups. My mother could hold me only so long before I'd start squirming, eager to get to the floor and experience life on my own. With that much innate energy, it was no wonder that at age fifty-one I should have broken through the limitations of a sub–3:30 time set for women forty and over, in order to qualify for my first Boston Marathon.

When I was just two, I had my first swim. My family was at a summer resort off Lake Michigan, and Daddy took me out on a pier, intending to let me down over the side for a gentle dunk. He became momentarily distracted watching a sailboat. Before he knew it, I had wiggled free of his grasp and beat him to the plunge. He immediately dove in after me and managed to grab hold of a limb, expecting to find me gasping and sobbing. To his surprise, I emerged giggling, as if I'd put something over on him. I have never had a fear of water, even though some perilous adventures were to follow.

When I was nine, we took a family vacation at Black Lake, which feeds into Lake Michigan. Since Daddy's days as a champion oarsman had ended, he decided to try his hand at sailing. My mother suggested we rent a boat with a skipper for the first time out. Daddy reluctantly acquiesced, but stood by the tiller as we left port. We were nearing the end of our sail when a gust of wind took the skipper by surprise. He shifted the sail quickly enough to keep us from dipping into the water, but was not fast enough to dodge the boom. He got a fair-sized gash on his forehead. Luckily, he was still conscious and able to instruct Daddy how to maneuver the boat into the harbor. After my father did this successfully, it just whetted his appetite for solo sailing. Within a week, he wanted to go out again, this time without a skipper. My mother was still apprehensive, and decided to leave my three-year-old younger brother with the nurse. Daddy was determined that we wear our life preservers. I insisted I knew how to swim, but he did not relent.

Before boarding, Daddy issued some orders: "No matter what happens," he warned my older brother and me, "just keep sitting. Don't move!" Before long, we were out in the middle of the lake, a good distance from shore. The weather was cool and overcast. The wind had picked up, and Mommy pleaded, "Darling, it's getting a little chilly for the children. Don't you think we had better head in?" Daddy started to grumble something, but with the statement still stuck in his mouth, the wind hit us at an angle. Confused, he was uncertain which way to shift the jib. Whatever he did, it was wrong.

The boat tilted and slowly began to capsize. I found myself in the water, with the boat on top of me. I knew there was some reason why I had rejected the idea of wearing a life preserver! What good was it now when I was pinned under the boat? I didn't have much time to think. As the murkiness surrounded me, I knew I couldn't hold my breath forever. Suddenly, the inspiration hit: dive down and then come up from under the boat's edge. Though this maneuver was tricky enough without a vest, it was even more so with one. I managed to get out from under.

On the opposite side of the boat was Mommy, calling frantically to me, "Where is your brother?" I blurted, "I don't know. I guess he's pinned under the boat too!" She held on to the boat with one hand and reached under it with the other, trying to make contact. I was relieved to see her pull out an arm attached to my brother. His face was as gloomy as the sky, and I could read his thoughts: "Yeah! 'Don't move; just keep sitting; everything will be all right!'"

My father now ordered: "Hold on to the boat. The wind will push us to shore." As I clung to the boat, I noticed bits of apparel, such as my cap, and other remnants from the craft floating away in the chop. Also, I observed that the wind wasn't blowing us toward shore, that the boat was gradually sinking, and that there were concerned looks on my parents' faces.

I heard Mommy praying, while Daddy was trying to stay in control. I was being practical. I suggested, "If the boat is sinking, why don't we try to swim for shore?" Suggestion overruled! Daddy was at the nose of the boat facing the channel leading out to Lake Michigan, and spotted a Coast Guard boat coming through it a good distance off. Would they notice us? My mother's prayers increased, the Coast Guard cutter kept coming closer and we were hopeful we had been spotted. Not too soon, either, as the boat to which we had been clinging was nearly submerged. Prayers answered.

We later found out that the Coast Guard just happened to be on routine lookout since it was so rough out on Lake Michigan.

They had no idea of what was happening on Black Lake until they were spirited toward us. Daddy concluded afterwards that he was a better oarsman than sailor, for there were no more invitations to go sailing.

Daddy went from being a sportsman to being a coach for his children, teaching me to ride my first two-wheeler at age seven, and then helping me get astride Mommy's green balloon-tired bike. Daddy held the bike to balance it and gave me instructions as he guided me forward. He proudly let go when he found I was handling it on my own momentum. I was elated by my new accomplishment. We moved on to roller-skating. In those days, we had old-fashioned clamp-on skates. I was just beginning to master the crossover for taking corners, when one skate broke loose in the middle of such a move. To this day, I have tell-tale scars on my right knee.

Saint Louis had cold, snowy winters when I was young, and before going to bed on Christmas Eve, we kept peeking out the windows to watch for the carolers and to see if it had started snowing. On one Christmas, Santa surprised us with a sled. The first time Daddy took my brother and me sledding, my mother stayed home with my four-month-old brother. It was cold out, and even though we were warmly wrapped with mittens and mufflers, it did not take long for the cold to penetrate and the numbness to set in. Daddy, eager to get the most mileage out of our new Nordic conveyance, seemed oblivious to the temperature. Even our hesitancy to follow him up the hill for "one more time" didn't register with him, though it did when we got home and he experienced our mother's reaction when she looked at us. Sheepishly, he left the scene while Mommy pulled off our mittens, jackets, boots, and stockings as she warned us that the water she was pouring over us would hurt for awhile and that it would feel hot even though it was room temperature.

Our first experience of frostbite didn't hamper our enjoyment of that lovely white stuff. Next winter, we were eager to try out Art Hill, so named because the Saint Louis Art Museum was perched at the top. It sloped down to the lagoon in Forest Park, which froze in the winter.

Sled perched on the crest of the hill, Daddy took the rear with the two of us packed in front of him, steering with his feet. The next time down, he decided we should pile on top of him, stomach first. He steered with his arms, having just enough strength to turn us sharply at the bottom of the hill, barely in time to avoid going over the embankment onto the frozen lagoon. Three of us on the sled made things a bit wobbly, so Daddy suggested that we two children try it alone. I was to be on the bottom to do the steering, as I was older and taller. My brother was instructed to pile on top of me.

Speeding down the hill, I found I didn't have sufficient control. We hit a bump midway that acted as a catapult for the sled. I could not turn at the bottom in time. There was little I could do when my brother yelled, "We're heading straight for the lagoon!" It was at least a three-foot drop onto solid ice. Fortunately it didn't break under our impact, but I had the breath knocked out of me. When my brother and I got over the ringing in our ears and the stars dancing before our eyes, we looked each other over and passed inspection. No broken bones! The sled, however, was never quite the same.

At the family dinner table, it was my father's ritual to listen to the six o'clock news on the radio while we ate. *The Lone Ranger* followed. Until this was over, we were held to sacred silence, while my father stood at the head of the table, listening intently, wielding the carving knife with dexterity. One evening, I had turned to whisper something to my brother when my father, instead of asking which slice I wanted, tapped me on the arm with the two-pronged carving fork to get my attention. Unmindful of the implement, I turned suddenly to see what he wanted. Imagine my surprise to find the carving fork stuck in my arm. I don't know who was more shocked, my father or myself. "Sit still, don't move!" he commanded. "This won't hurt." He skillfully pressed his fingers between the prongs against my flesh, and withdrew the fork as abruptly as it had entered. This episode was more exciting than *The Lone Ranger* and broke the silence. His apologies were profuse.

Mommy was the pacifier who tempered my father when he unleashed his authority, and I was very attached to her—so much so that I didn't want to go to school when the time came. She had been playing school with both my brother and me, introducing us to books and paper, until we reached the age to go to kindergarten, and I saw no reason to leave. My brother, though, seemed eager to head out. Perhaps he welcomed some space from his older sister, who tended to be a bit overbearing in her role as second mama. Following in my father's footsteps, as well, I often became the on-the-scene defense attorney, meting out justice to my brothers when the three of them argued.

One evening my father came home from a hard day at the office and rolled up the driveway just in time to see the stained-glass window at the bottom of our staircase suddenly shatter in front of him onto the driveway. He rushed into the house, where he found my three-year-old brother crouched under the ill-fated window, and grabbed him by the nape of his neck. I started yell-

ing, "Stop it, Daddy. Stop it! He didn't do it!" My father halted
momentarily, stunned by my vehemence. I yelled that it was my
older brother who was at fault. He'd thrown the ball from the
top of the stairs, meaning to hit my younger brother, who was
smart enough to duck. "You should get after him instead," I said.
Ordinarily I would not have had the nerve to tell my father what
to do, but my fear of possible repercussions was overridden by
my desire to see justice served. My father relinquished his grip
on my younger brother and did not use his heavy hand on me. I
learned how speaking up can make a difference.

Before bed, I knelt with my mother for prayers, and at the end
of the litany of blessings, I added, ". . . and please bless Mommy
and let me die before her!" At this early age, I could not conceive
of life without her. Having heard this several times, she finally
decided it was time to talk to me. I must have been satisfied with
her reasoning, for I stopped repeating this prayer.

Outdoor activities attracted me more than the indoor. When I
took piano lessons, my thoughts were racing outside, where I
longed to be, rather than being perched on a bench for half an
hour trying to read musical notes. In ballet class, my tall, lanky
body felt awkward. Even though I yearned for a pair of pink
toe shoes all my own, I became disenchanted when I found it
hurt to stand on my toes. Plus, it was just too unnatural to walk
en pointe when I was already tall enough. I'd rather be climbing
trees, jumping rope, playing cops 'n' robbers, kick the can, hop-
scotch, or just running around.

If my grandfather had wanted a boy, he had a tomboy in me.
Even though I was a second mother to my brothers, I was also

their companion and, if anything went wrong, an umpire and protector. True to my Leo sign, I was a fighter when necessary. When two neighborhood bullies threatened to interrupt our gang at play, I suggested we beat it to the back porch and lock ourselves inside. But my brother didn't move fast enough, and the two bullies grabbed him. I bolted out the front door of our neighbors' house and surprised my brother's captors by yelling, "Let my brother go!" I doubled my fist and planted it squarely in the oldest boy's left eye, and as the assailant winced from the blow, I pulled my brother out of his grip. After that, we were no longer bothered.

When my mother gave birth to her fourth child, I was hoping for a little sister. My two younger brothers had each other, and I wanted a playmate of my own. Alas! This child too turned out to be a boy. Nonetheless, I treated him as if he were my little sister. One day, when he was three, I dressed him in one of my white slips for a tea party and was tying a wide pink ribbon around his waist when my eldest brother passed by the door, did a double take, and glared. "What are you letting her do to you?" My little companion looked at me, looked at his brother, and trotted off after him. There went my "little sister." What was I to do?

I had never liked playing with dolls, though my maternal grandmother encouraged me, teaching me to cut and sew doll clothes, but I wanted something alive. A playmate down the block had a darling buff cocker spaniel named Taffy, and when my twelfth birthday was coming up I began dropping hints to my mother. I stuck a picture of a red cocker, clipped from *Life* magazine, on my bedroom door and printed *Winkie* under the picture. I'd chosen the name from a book I was reading about a carrier pigeon in World War II by that name, and thought it fit the perky red spaniel.

On the morning I turned twelve, my mother knocked softly on my door. "Are you awake, darling?" She came into my room carrying a bow-topped basket. In a lilting voice she said, "Happy Birthday," placing the basket at the foot of my bed. Out popped a little cocker spaniel puppy who snuggled right up to me under the covers. Winkie and I became inseparable. She was a real Godsend because, as it turned out, I really needed a friend at the time. I was changing schools and having a tough time.

Up until fifth grade, I was a carefree spirit. I didn't have home-work. I was going to a public school, and you simply learned by osmosis, according to the Dewey system. The educators thought when you were ready to learn, you would. I can remember sit-ting at my desk in the fifth grade, doing nothing and looking up at the alphabet cards pinned around the eaves of the classroom when it occurred to me that I didn't know those things in order. How could I use the dictionary or phone book if I didn't? In ten minutes, I had the letters memorized.

In fourth grade, we had studied American history. I enjoyed the candle-making from scratch, the butter-churning, and mak-ing soap out of lye just as our forebears had, but I didn't feel like playing house in the cabin—especially since I'd been paired with a "husband" not of my own choosing. This was pushing it too far, I thought, so I went to my desk and pulled out my history book to see what it had to say. It read like a storybook, and I became absorbed. This is how my reading began to pick up. Until this point, I much preferred listening to my mother read out loud, and to her dramatizations of historical events.

In sixth grade, I was still in public school, and my classmates were beginning to have boy-and-girl parties. I went to a few parties, and after each, my parents would discreetly ask me what we'd done. Naively, I gave an account of the games we played, a few of which involved kissing as a token reward.

My parents pricked up their ears and decided it would be better to send me to an all-girls school instead of explaining to me about the birds and the bees. At that point, my only information had come from a chalk drawing in the driveway. When I was eight or nine, a friend whose father was a doctor chalked a picture for my brother and me to see. I couldn't believe this drawing of a private part was an accurate depiction of sexual anatomy, but my brother backed her up knowingly. Stunned, I wondered where he'd gotten his information. After all, he was thirteen months younger than I was.

When I later approached my mother, she offered a watered-down version of intercourse that left me confused and none the wiser. I decided the whole subject was too distasteful to bring up again, and Mommy must have felt she'd done her duty, because it was not until I was nearing thirteen that the topic was revisited in a bit more detail, and this because I was beginning to double date.

When I was pulled out of public school, Mommy succeeded in getting Daddy's permission for us to have formal religious instruction. Up until then, Daddy had reneged on his promise to let Mommy rear us as Catholics. He had made the promise because in those days, the Roman Catholic Church didn't allow its members to marry non-Catholics unless the couple agreed to bring up their children in the Catholic Church. My grandmother, wise woman that she was, advised my mother to wait until we had grown older to be formally instructed as Catholics, but to baptize us herself at home. Should anything unforeseen happen, we would still be sealed as children of God.

When I was ten years old, Mommy took my two older brothers and me to receive formal instruction in the Catholic faith at Visitation Academy, where she and my grandmother had both been educated by the nuns. For me, the academy was a forbidding medieval structure. Built of red brick, it had a cupola complete with belfry, copper guttering green with age, and gargoyles perched atop the high portal guarding the entrance. Inside, it was a maze of long, dark corridors with a musty smell.

The warmth of the Sister who taught us helped to compensate for the surroundings. After a month or two of lessons, we were ready to receive the Sacrament of Baptism. This took place in Saint Louis University College Church. I remember the feeling of newness and freshness that came upon me, and I announced to my Catholic neighbors afterwards, "I feel I'm all God's now. He has His hands on me." When they asked my oldest brother what he felt, his answer was, "Nothing." I couldn't believe what I was hearing, since we both had received the same sacrament.

Scarcely a week later, we returned to Visitation Academy to make our First Communion. My youngest brother, only three and a half at the time, was up in the gallery with the Sister who had instructed us. Instead of following the proceedings, he was attracted by the winged cherubs on the high arched ceiling and, in his youthful imagination, envisioned shooting them down.

With rifle-like gestures and audible sounds, he began picking them off. Though we were temporarily distracted by his antics and Sister's semisuppressed snickering, the ceremony resumed and I received Jesus into my heart.

Now came a difficult decision. My parents gave me the choice between going to school at Visitation Academy or another private school where the society in Saint Louis sent their daughters. Neither place appealed to me. Visitation seemed like a dungeon; the other school seemed snobbish. After much agonizing, I chose the dungeon over the snobs.

At twelve years old, I entered uncharted waters—uniforms, regimen, homework, all girls! My grandfather was not pleased with my choice of school because it meant dealing with Catholics, for whom he had no fondness. But midway through my first year, I overheard him saying to my parents, "Well, that 'Hesitation Convent'"—as he liked to call it—"seems to be making a lady of her after all!"

The first day I walked into seventh grade, Sister Consolata was at the board diagramming sentences. I looked around the room and everyone seemed to know what she was talking about except me. I had never heard of grammar, let alone diagramming. When she gave out the homework, I sat at my desk and began to sob. Sister came to my side. "What's the matter, dear?" I explained that I hadn't understood a thing she'd said, and that I'd never had homework before. She told me to come to study hall, and she would help me.

"Study hall?" I gulped. "When do I get to play?" In study

hall, we had to take our seats silently and not murmur a word for a whole hour. But Sister gave me the help I needed. It didn't take long for the influence of the Sisters to begin shaping my future. Their chanting at vespers and the incense at Benediction drew me to the chapel regularly in the afternoon before I went to study hall. I felt a special relationship with the Virgin Mary. What more powerful intermediary can we have than the Blessed Mother?

At home, I set up a little altar table in my bedroom, and would sit there in the darkness after dinner to meditate. At first Mommy took offense, feeling shut out. Then she attributed it to a passing phase; but it concerned her enough that she brought up the subject of motherhood to me, and told me about the joys of breastfeeding a child. Sensing that I was being drawn to the Sisterhood, she mentioned that I hadn't even dated yet. How quickly she had reversed herself from the mother who had yanked me out of public school because there was too much boy–girl interaction at parties!

The nuns' influence was so prevailing that they even charmed me out of my stage fright. In elementary school, I had been mortified during the first-grade Easter pageant when the powder puff serving as my bunny tail fell off and the audience began laughing. But by the eighth grade, when the Sisters presented me with the female lead in our graduation play, *Lady Windermere's Fan*, I thoroughly enjoyed it.

Four years later I landed the lead ingénue in the all-girl cast of *The Rivals*, our high school graduation play. When I saw some of my girlfriends struggling to be convincing in their male roles, I did a little coaching on the side. After all, I had three brothers! I suppose by now I had also acquired some of my mother's talent for acting and was no longer inhibited about appearing before an audience. As I projected myself into the roles, I lost my self-consciousness, a good lesson for life: Take the focus off of yourself and concentrate on something else.

3

Coming of Age

If we are in any way to succeed,
we must heed the little voice within.

By FOURTEEN, I knew what I wanted to do with my life, but
I figured I would date and play the field, if only to prove that
it would not affect my decision. By ninth grade, I had a best
friend with two attractive brothers. We were spending weekends
at each other's houses. Pretty soon we were double-dating, usually with one of her brothers, and I was never without something
to do or someone to do it with over the weekends.

My grandfather began noticing my popularity and often inquired, "Well, who was it this time?" If he didn't hear the same
boy's name mentioned too frequently, he was relieved. "There's
safety in numbers," he'd say. I knew what he meant, and that's
the way I wanted it too. In my heart, I had secret plans.

By then, I had become an accomplished equestrian. My
brothers and I had been introduced to horseback riding because

my mother's chiropractor thought it would help her back, and my oldest brother and I were expected to accompany her. Eventually, two of my brothers got involved in racing over jumps on steeplechase courses. I fashioned the silks that my oldest brother wore by sewing red and yellow stripes on a background of white. This was my sole participation in that sport. My preference was riding three- and five-gaited show horses, but on occasion I joined the foxhunts, which were followed by hunt breakfasts at private homes.

At one of these events, when I was sixteen and in my junior year at Visitation, I met a young medical intern named Tom Dooley. He was studying for his medical degree at Saint Louis University. He had a gift for the piano and also competed in the jumping classes at horse shows. We'd sit together at the shows awaiting his event, which was often last. Around Christmastime, Tom talked me into making Christmas stockings for the children's ward at Deaconess Hospital, where he interned. Then he insisted I come and help distribute them. I sensed that he wanted to show off his lady friend to the kids. When I saw the adoring look in the children's eyes as Tom talked with them, treating them with great gentleness and sensitivity, I had a new respect for him. Still, I was not attracted to him as a mate for life.

Our dating came to an abrupt end when he arrived to pick me up one evening and I wasn't ready. I was still sewing on the outfit I intended to wear and kept him waiting half an hour chatting with my parents. Ordinarily, he enjoyed this, but tonight he remarked to them, "Does she think she's the only girl in town?" He brightened up when he saw me coming down the stairs in the red wool flare skirt I'd just completed. We had a pleasant evening, but there were no more dates. I had a number of other suitors on the string, and Tom was getting ready to enter the service as a medic, so calling it off was mutual and didn't bother me in the least.

By now, I knew that no man was able to fill the recesses of my heart like God himself. My experience with the nuns at school had begun to foster a new interior life that was strengthening me. I was thirteen when I studied the Catechism in order to receive the Sacrament of Confirmation. For me it was no chore, but a delight. After Confirmation as a full-fledged Christian, I felt ready to conquer the world for Christ. Little did I realize then, as I do now, that the real battle in life is in conquering self.

I had become artful at warding off good-night kisses at the door. If I sensed a serious intent toward the end of the evening, I came up with some sort of creative distraction. I concentrated on my studies and continued to ride and show my horse, Wally Highland. Many times I came home from the stables and took off my sweaty jodhpurs to find the insides of my knees rubbed raw. All of this I simply took in stride as the necessary sacrifices to achieving a goal.

One of Wally Highland's most popular events was the combination class, where I showed her under harness first, then stripped her, saddled her and put her through her gaited paces. The music and applause stimulated her, and she would put on a fine performance. But she always got restless in the lineup, waiting for the judges' decision. She would whirl around, sidestep, or rear, endangering the photographers. It was a challenge for me to hold her steady with one hand and reach down to accept the trophy with the other. When I was sixteen, I won the Grand

Championship at the Maryville Horse Show, an annual fund-raising event for that all-girl's college in Saint Louis, which I was soon to attend.

By the time I was eighteen and in school at Maryville College, I had met a man, a young Irishman three years older than I, who was not so easily dissuaded. I was attracted to him, which took me quite off guard and sent me into an emotional spin that made me realize I had to come to grips with my situation. I was at the crossroads, and I knew it—whether to marry or enter the Convent? I couldn't keep playing the social butterfly forever. He wanted to force me into a decision, and even presented a written proposal by offering me his diary to read. What an eye-opener! We definitely connected on a spiritual level, enough so that he detected my religious leanings, but he was unwilling to accept my desire to enter the religious life until he had showed his hand. I was very flattered, frightened, and confused. Was this another temptation to make me swerve from my course, or was God actually trying to redirect me?

One April afternoon when I returned from my classes, my mother announced she had something serious to tell me. Cushion it as she might, nothing prepared me for the shock of Wally Highland's death. It was sudden and unanticipated: The horse had reared in her stall as if catapulted by pain, and had fallen, writhing, to the floor. By the time the vet arrived, there was nothing he could do. She had died of a cerebral hemorrhage. We later wondered whether the condition that led to her death might have accounted for her touchiness at the trophy lineup.

After a week's mourning, I decided this was the signal to end my equestrian showmanship. Gently but firmly, I was being summoned by the Lord to prepare myself for the life to which

I had been called five years earlier at the age of fourteen. I was gradually being divested of my worldly attachments. So as not to raise suspicion regarding my life's choice, I continued to date, but I was on guard to make sure that nothing would develop to dissuade me.

In my second year at Maryville, I was invited to the Notre Dame prom, so I cut my Friday classes and took the train to South Bend. Although I had a great time, it did not sit well with the Madame of the Sacred Heart that I had skipped classes because of a social occasion. I argued that I had never used my quota of sick days, and had assumed I had a day or two coming. She insisted such days were not to be used for a "frivolous function."

Since there was not a meeting of the minds, I decided to please Daddy and transfer to his alma mater, Washington University, for the remaining two years of college. It was a shock, however, to find myself at a secular university, being rushed by sorority sisters, courted by fraternity men, nominated for ROTC queen, and pressured to choose a major. I decided on drama since I came by it naturally, being my mother's daughter. I later switched to elementary education, but kept drama as my minor.

My Irishman, who was Catholic and studying architecture, began making inroads where no one else had been allowed to trespass. Despite my intentions, I was becoming vulnerable in an area I had sequestered for God alone. We attended Mass, lectures, dinners, dances, concerts, and operas together often. We went for long Sunday drives and spent quiet evenings at my family home. My grandfather began to hear this young man's name mentioned frequently and was eventually introduced. The fact that the young man was Catholic was one strike against him, but being Irish made it two. Somewhere in my grandfather's past, he had had unfortunate dealings with a priest, who most likely was also Irish. Still, my friend humored my grandfather in such a way that he gained his respect.

After my sophomore year, I attended summer school at the University of Wisconsin. When the session was over, I joined my family for a vacation. We took in Wyoming, including Devil's Tower, Jackson Hole, and the Grand Tetons. We spent a night in Spearfish, South Dakota, and went to the famous Passion Play about the life of Christ, performed there every ten years. How fortunate that we happened to hit the right year.

It was a beautiful starlit night as we sat in the open amphitheater, where the processions were complete with live camels, horses, donkeys, and oxen on an expansive outdoor stage. The Crucifixion scene took place on a hill to our right. The hammering of the nails resounding through the stillness of the night echoed in my heart. The climax for me was God's own theatrics. Just at the precise moment when Christ's body was being lowered from the cross on a winding sheet, a shooting star arched over the scene in the dark backdrop of night. I was awestruck.

I could still remember pondering the mystery of the Crucifixion at age five when Mommy had finished this portion of our Lenten Sunday school lesson. Shortly afterwards, I was sitting at the top of the steps sobbing when she noticed me and asked what was wrong. "I don't see how he could do it!" I sobbed.

"Who? Do what?" she wanted to know.

"The Father let his Son die like that," I said, "especially if he

loved him so." She gently talked to me about the concept of sacrifice. Even so, it was some time before I was able to understand
the words she quoted, from John: "No greater love than this can
a man have than to lay down his life for another."

Now, as I sat under the stars in the amphitheater, I realized
I was on the threshold of doing just that with my own life. In
renouncing the pleasures of the world, I wanted nothing more
than the conversion of my father and grandfather to the Catholic
faith that I revered. In the end, I wanted all of us to be united in
one faith.

4

Stepping Out in Faith

Any worthwhile undertaking involves sacrifice.

LOOKING BACK ON my life, I see two profound events that changed everything—one that I planned with determination, the other that occurred quite by circumstance. Both threw me into unknown territory. The first event occurred on December 8, 1956, in historic Saint Nicholas Abbey in Angers, France, when I pronounced my final vows. I was now a fully fledged member of the Sisters of the Good Shepherd.

I was twenty-six, and returned to the United States to receive my assignment, working with troubled girls. I had spent three years in preparation for a life of faith, and now it had become a reality. This had been my desire since age fourteen. Although I thought I would be cloistered for the rest of my life, I had no idea that in joining a semicloistered Order I would be required to travel so much. After a number of moves, I eventually settled in Spokane, Washington.

In 1978, another event occurred that was just as drastic, but unplanned. I was introduced to running, and I'll never forget it. I can still conjure up the feel of my feet moving over the sandy beach, the sense of absolute freedom. It happened while I was attending a workshop on spirituality at Rockaway, on the Oregon coast. I was just about to have my forty-eighth birthday and had been a Catholic nun for more than two decades.

During an informal conversation at the retreat, Father John Topel, who was connected at the time with Gonzaga University in Spokane, began talking about the benefits of running. He mentioned what a joyful release it was to harmonize mind, body, and soul. He went on to explain how running helped diminish depression, diabetes, addictions, stress, increase concentration, and so forth.

"Nothing could be that good," I told him. "I have been active all my life, and I always enjoyed sports. But I can't just get out there and run for no good reason. I need a goal." Father smiled and looked out at the beach. "In that case, go out and run between those two eddies without getting wet."

Later that evening, I found a pair of running shorts in a pile of clothing that had been donated to the girls under our care, and I put on a pair of secondhand tennis shoes given to me by a former sister-in-law. Just to test the priest's theories, I set out running in the dark between the two eddies. It felt good and not burdensome at all. Father Topel spotted me as I returned and asked where I had been. "Oh, out there, doing what you suggested." He nodded his approval and asked how far I had gone.

"Between those two eddies," was my response.

"Do you know how far that is?"

"Yes, about half a mile."

"Right you are. How often did you stop?"

"I didn't."

Then he asked how long it had taken me.

"About five minutes."

He seemed impressed and said, "Good. You must keep it up now!"

Running seemed to come naturally, so I kept going. I had a couple more days at the beach so I went for a run each day, since Father had emphasized the need for consistency. Never did I realize at the time what the consequences would be. Like everything else I engaged in, I just stepped out in faith.

Six months before, I had seen a TV movie called *See How She Runs* about a middle-aged school teacher, played by Joanne Woodward, who aspired to run the Boston Marathon. At the time, that race meant nothing to me. I was merely impressed by the story of her uphill battle and the fortitude it took to withstand the ridicule from her family and her students while she suffered the rigors of intensive training.

When she finally made it to the Boston Marathon, I saw something deeper in her struggles. In one scene in the movie, someone in the crowd hands her a towel to wipe the sweat from her face. I thought immediately of Veronica using her veil to wipe the bloody sweat from Jesus's face while he was carrying the cross. In the film, the sun goes down, the other runners have crossed the finish line, and Woodward's character has reached the point of exhaustion. Still, she plows on, only to fall. The agony on her face as she forces herself to get up exemplified for me the Christ figure. The richness of this symbolic expression never left me. Her faith seemed to me equivalent to Jesus dragging the cross to Calvary for our sakes. Little did I realize that one day I would be participating in this same race for the sake of another.

It was April 1, 1978, when I took my first run on the beach. Yes, I became a fool for Christ on April Fool's day. Five weeks later I tried my first race. But why? What made me do it? I had found a cause. "Quitters never win and winners never quit," my grandfather had often admonished me. Maybe that too was part of it.

When I got home to Spokane, I decided to keep running. At our Convent there was a ball field used by the girls in our care, so I took to running around it. A week later I was coming out of a photo shop where I developed my own photographs when I noticed a poster on the window advertising something called the "second annual Bloomsday run," an 8.2-mile race. The poster depicted a crowd of people running elbow to elbow. Who would want to do such a thing? It's hard enough to work up enough energy to run by yourself without having to elbow your way through a herd of runners. Yet the more I resisted the idea, the more it clung to me.

That evening I received a call from my mother, who gently tried to break the news that one of my brothers seemed to be headed toward divorce most probably due to an alcoholic problem. All of a sudden I blurted, "That settles it. I'm going to do it."

"Do what, darling?" was my mother's puzzled response.

I told her that I would run the Bloomsday race as a Living Way of the Cross, hoping that the Lord would accept my willingness to endure hardship and transfer this strength to my brother, so that he could overcome his dependency on alcohol and be able to restore his marriage.

"Oh my," said my mother, "how far is this race?" Now my poor mother had another reason to be concerned.

"It's 8.2 miles," I told her. As I pronounced these words, the idea sounded awful to me too.

"But darling," she said, horrified. "You can't do that. Certainly you haven't been trained for that."

"Only God knows. How will I know unless I try?" I responded as we hung up. I was resolved to do it no matter what the cost. I promised God I would struggle through the event for my brother. I prayed that God would honor my desire and help my brother with his problems.

I started training even though I had no idea what training was. For the next couple of weeks, I was harder on my body than I have ever been in my entire life. I continued running around the girls' ball field at our complex. In my second week, I had worked up to twenty-eight laps around the perimeter of the field, which I figured was about seven miles. Tired of running in circles, I took to running on concrete sidewalks. I was still wearing my secondhand tennis shoes with thin soles, and I was running in long pants that flapped at my ankles.

After another week of this, my calves were so tight I couldn't even make an indentation when I pressed my fingers against them. My knees were so enlarged I could scarcely bend them.

Worse was the overall exhaustion and the forced pattern of breathing, which I had not counted on. I knew nothing about warm-ups or cool-downs. I kept pushing on, but into the third week, I broke down, hid in my room, and started crying. "I can't, Lord," I sobbed, "I can't. I know I promised, but I just can't. My whole body is rebelling."

When I finally quieted down, I heard a voice coming from

my depths. "I know you are stepping out in faith, not knowing what the end results of your efforts will be, but I too had to step out in faith, complying with my Father's will, not knowing how many people down through the ages would respond to my supreme act of love by laying down my life for them."

"All right, Lord, you win, but I can't do it alone. You will have to be my strength." Finally I wrestled myself loose from the bed, hobbled down the steps and out the side door. Doing that took all my willpower. When I got back from the run, I felt no worse for wear; but then, how could I? I had already hit bottom. "Thank you, God," I prayed, "for letting me get through this effort."

Now I had but one week left before the race. A benefactor of the Convent found out what I was intending to do and was appalled that I had no running shoes. He insisted on taking me shopping. It took us quite a bit of looking to find shoes that were narrow enough for my foot. In those days there were no widths or half sizes for running shoes. The saleswoman was good enough to discount them because of the "nonprofit organization" to which I belonged, so I was a little bit more reconciled to the expenditure of $12.99. The shoes were multicolored and made me feel as if I were wearing boats on my feet. Plus, breaking them in soon added to my woes. Entering into the 8.2-mile run after only five weeks of training with enlarged knees and tightened calves was bad enough. Now I also had blisters.

Race day came, a bright and clear May day of seventy degrees—my kind of weather. The camaraderie in the back ranks made the event seem festive as we ran through the streets of Spokane. At first I had only one goal, just to get through the race, and that would be it. But by the time I reached the finish line, I realized that I couldn't let go of running. The experience certainly taught me a lot I hadn't known about running, but also about myself. I was amazed at how much a body can endure, but also at how much training was required to complete the run.

I vowed never to put my body through the torture of that kind of amateur conditioning again. I had also realized that if you are going to kill yourself, you might as well do it for a cause. After the race, I went down to the Spokane River and waded in the cold water to help heal my legs. I had not planned on doing this, but when I saw the water, somehow I knew it would soothe my throbbing muscles. Instinctively my body was telling me what to do for itself. I truly think it is this instinct that has allowed me to survive all the subsequent years of competition.

At the end of the Bloomsday race, the organizers were passing out entry forms for other races. My first thought was that I didn't ever want to put myself through that agony again. So as to avoid it I would just have to keep going. I already had these crazy looking running shoes and might as well get some use out of them. I decided to just enter one race a month. That's how it all began.

All I knew at the time was that I was running on faith, and I prayed while I ran. Afterwards, I realized it was a different kind of prayer posture. Besides using my heart and head, when I ran my whole body was involved in the petitioning. I had no idea what effect my running prayers might eventually have on my brother's life, but somehow I knew I was being transformed by it myself.

To this day I don't know if I made the right choice to run for my brother. But this I do know: Running Bloomsday was for me a form of prayer, and prayers are always answered, although not always in the way we might expect. I knew my efforts wouldn't be in vain, but that the outcome might be far different than the one for which I had hoped. God has a divine sense of humor and has plans of His own, sometimes initiating surprises. Ultimately, my running had no effect on saving my brother from divorce. He did, however, remarry—the second time to a Baptist who did not tolerate drinking. In her presence, at least, he abstained.

That first race made me aware of my possibilities as a runner, surprised by being fourth out of 300 in my age group. Up to this point, I knew next to nothing about the sport. I knew that it required putting one foot in front of the other at a quickened pace so that at least one foot was in the air at all times. But running itself had not been part of the athletic curriculum in my day, even though I had engaged in a number of other sports that required running, including field hockey, basketball, baseball, running high jump, tennis, soccer, and ordinary neighborhood games. I enjoyed all of these, held my own fairly well, and was on some winning teams, acquiring my share of ribbons.

Now that I had become a confirmed runner at age forty-eight, I knew I might be considered out of the ordinary by some. When I began running in 1978, running had yet to be embraced by a generation beyond the baby boomers. Back then, most of my race companions were considerably younger than I was. I also realized I would need to keep vigilant. The more gifts we have, the more responsibility we have to keep everything in balance. Running creates a feeling of wholeness, and when it is there, I feel at peace with myself and others. But as I was about to find out, keeping things in balance and achieving that sense of wholeness would be harder than I imagined.

5

Peaks and Valleys

Not to risk is not to live fully.

ONCE I BEGAN running and competing, I rediscovered my adventurous spirit, which as a young woman had led me to some precarious places.

After my junior year in college, I went to summer school at the University of Colorado in Boulder, where I had my first taste of mountain climbing. When traveling out West, I always had felt drawn by mountains, but never had the opportunity to climb one. But one day, in Boulder, an Austrian fellow from a neighboring fraternity house invited me to scale Arapaho Glacier.

I happily set out, having no idea that we'd be crossing over snowfields, nor that the temperature could change dramatically with altitude. I was wearing loafers, the only shoes I had, and shorts, but luckily had been warned to bring some outer clothing. It was bright and sunny when we began, but the sensation of sinking into snow up to my hips in shorts was new, and there was no way to keep my shoes dry. Soon the Austrian suggested I slip into my long pants. This made climbing a bit more tedious, but by the time we had ascended, I was wrapped in scarf and jacket.

I will never forget the awe that engulfed me as I sat perched on top of the world. We couldn't tarry. My guide was wise enough to know that we needed to maintain our warmth by staying on the move, although like Peter, James, and John atop Mount Tabor, I would have loved to have lingered longer. Invigorated by the exertion and enthralled with the rarified air, my head was still in the clouds even when my body was back to base. I couldn't wait to climb another mountain.

For my senior year, I returned to Washington University, and when I graduated my parents arranged a promised trip to Europe. My Irishman, meanwhile, had graduated from Notre Dame with a degree in architecture and had enlisted in the Marines. He'd been assigned to the East Coast, and I felt that God had had a hand in this arrangement, because it gave me some distance.

Accompanied by seven girls who'd graduated with me, I set out for Europe. We referred to ourselves as "the unholy eight" in anticipation of an audience that had been arranged with His Holiness Pope Pius XII. We were to embark for Europe by ship from Quebec via the Saint Lawrence River, and since my Irishman was in Rhode Island, I went ahead several days earlier than my friends to visit with him. My grandmother came along as chaperone. She was fond of my friend too, and the fact that he was a Catholic was definitely in his favor. She was of French extraction and an ardent Catholic.

While at Notre Dame my Irishman had met a Holy Cross priest who had become his spiritual mentor, and who had been transferred to the Holy See in Rome as a Canon lawyer. This Monsignor Doheny insisted that my Irishman introduce the girl of his choice before any romantic plans were hatched. He told me how to contact the Monsignor while I was in Rome. Reluctantly, I promised to do so, although this was sounding far too serious for me!

While my Irishman and I were sitting in his car overlooking the Newport shoreline on the coast of Rhode Island, he began searching for something, muttering, "That's strange. I can't find it, and I just had it." He seemed perturbed.

"If I knew what it was, maybe I could help you look," I said, but I was almost afraid to hear the answer.

"It was something I wanted to give you," he said. "Well, you might as well know ... it was my graduation ring from Notre Dame. I wanted you to wear it, at least while you were gone, as a promise ring."

I said a quick, quiet prayer: "Please, Lord, don't let him find it, at least not now!" The move was too premature, too binding, and I didn't know how to handle it. The ring stayed lost, and I accepted its disappearance as a small sign that Providence was doing the directing. I was assuming that the interview with the Monsignor would help me reach a decision as well.

As I stood on the ship and waved good-bye, I was wearing the Saint Christopher medal my mother had given me, but no ring. My Irishman waved back, looking sad, and my grandmother had tears in her eyes. The ship churned through the waters of the Saint

Lawrence, heading toward the open ocean of the Atlantic, as I wondered what lay ahead.

We toured Paris first and then made our way to Rome, where we met with His Holiness Pope Pius XII and had our pictures taken with him. He conferred a special blessing upon us and our families. Next was my meeting with Monsignor Doheny. My appointment was meant to be only twenty minutes, but when the time was up, he told me to stay and pray, that he'd be back after attending to some business, so our session stretched into two hours. I told Monsignor Doheny of my early inclinations toward a spiritual life, and how that desire had grown over time, to the point that I had begun contemplating life as a Catholic Sister. And yet I'd also been drawn into a romance.

After much listening and discerning, he said that he believed I was, indeed, headed for a vocation in the Religious Life. This was not what I expected to hear from him, and it made me realize that my secular romantic flair had, in fact, been gaining strength. On the other hand, I was not ready to make a commitment to marriage while my heart was still yearning to make God the center of my life. Now his words shook my emotional moorings and left me exhausted.

The following day, quite by chance—or was it something more?—the Monsignor reached me by telephone in the lobby of our hotel. He wanted a follow-up appointment. We met again, and I departed from this visit bewildered and dazed, feeling my own uncertainties rise to the surface, yet marveling that he could be so certain when he said, "I see that you really do have a calling to the Religious Life, and I recommend you consider the Sisters of Our Lady of Charity of the Good Shepherd of Angers." I felt a little twinge of resentment at this, since, if I did choose this vocation, I had set my heart on joining the Sisters of the Visitation, who had nurtured me through my high school years.

I had a lot to think about as our little troupe of eight left Rome for Switzerland. My emotions were really in turmoil, and when I returned to the hotel I broke down sobbing. My friends were alarmed because they had never seen me like this. I explained, "The Monsignor's discernment has turned my whole life around, and I haven't been able to come to grips with it yet."

On the second day in Switzerland we took a scenic cogwheel up to the snowcapped Jungfrau, one of the highest peaks in the Swiss Alps. I was so enthralled that I began exploring, and missed the scheduled trip down with my companions. That left me with an hour and a half wait for the next tram, so I decided to explore some more. Clad only in a pair of shorts, shirt, and saddle shoes, I struck out to climb the mountain on my own beyond the lookout. I was intent on getting up to a high point, where I anticipated there would be a breathtaking view of Interlaken from the opposite side.

It was late afternoon when I set out, and the looks and gestures I was getting from the descending parties were apparent warnings that I should be joining them on the way down. But I kept marching upward. When I was far above the others, I heard a sound resembling thunder. I realized it was an avalanche, but far enough away that I wasn't worried. I trudged on and was soon enveloped in misty snow clouds. The afternoon rays had faded, and the skies thickened menacingly. The temperature dropped. I was drastically underdressed for such a venture. I saw cracks in the white snow field, deep crevasses I would need to cross to get back down, and wondered how solid the banks would be on either side, assuming I could make a running broad jump to clear them. Then I remembered the avalanche I had seen. All this was making me uneasy. I began to pray. "Lord, please get me down. I don't want to worry my companions. I need to catch that last cog rail."

Wet, cold, and bedraggled, I arrived just in time to board the last tram. I found standing room only, but was so relieved to be on it I couldn't complain. I knew I could not have made it without Godly intervention. I remembered the medal I was wearing, given me by my mother before my departure. Perhaps Saint Christopher's intercession had also played a part. Packed between bodies on the tram, a couple noticed me and identified me as a fellow American. My saddle shoes and shorts must have been a dead giveaway. I now realized that only men and boys wore *lederhosen*—leather shorts—not women! They were kind enough to take me under their wing. How relieved my companions were to see me. The next day was my twenty-second birthday, and they had been saving a telegram that had arrived from home, in order to surprise me. What if I had never made it back?

In Munich, adventure of a different sort awaited. In college at Maryville, I had made friends with a girl named Rosemary Fuggar from Germany. We had kept up our friendship, and when she heard I was coming to Europe, she wanted to arrange a visit. She declined to come into Munich, so asked instead if I would take a train to Ulm, where someone would pick me up and drive me to her. Her directions seemed vague; but the other girls thought I shouldn't disappoint Rosemary, so I set off—in a foreign country, not knowing the language or where exactly I was going.

When I got off the train at the designated stop, a white-haired man in a black suit walked right up to me and said, "Rosemary! Come!"—meaning, I supposed, that he was going to take me to Rosemary. But when we got in his car, a black Ford Model T, there was no Rosemary. He spoke little English, and I spoke little German, so it was hard to keep a conversation going. Finally we drove into a town square and pulled up to a high, forest-green enclosure.

"Prince Fuggar," announced the driver. Fuggar, Rosemary's surname, sounded familiar; it was the "prince" part that had me puzzled. I thought it was a joke, until I was led up steep stone steps through a grand entrance and onto red-carpeted stairs. Suits of armor, flanking both sides of the staircase, stood frozen in salute.

A servant led me to my room. Immediately she drew my bath water and indicated she'd be back to bathe me. I tried to tell her this wasn't necessary. By the time she returned, I had washed up and was fully clothed. Seeing that I had completed my toilette, she beckoned me to follow her. We entered another spacious bedroom, then a bath chamber, and there was Rosemary sitting in the tub. What a strange way to greet a guest, I thought. Rosemary waved off the servant, and while I was helping her out of the tub, she explained that she had become a victim of spinal meningitis. At the time, there was no known cure, and doctors had given her just six months to live.

The two of us talked until the prince—her cousin, it turned out—returned from deer hunting and requested my company. He was a striking figure—tall, tanned, and dressed in a traditional gray-flannel German outfit embroidered in forest green. That evening at dinner marked the first time since her illness that Rosemary had come to the table, and the three of us were served a full eight-course feast, complete with beer and champagne. After dinner came cordials. I had to fight to stay awake after my tedious trip, a full meal, and an abundance of alcoholic beverages. The dinner had begun at eight o'clock, the fashionable dinner hour in Europe.

It was well after midnight before I could persuade them to show me the chapel they had mentioned, because I wanted to attend the 6:00 a.m. Mass. We wound through long, narrow corridors, through heavy, squeaky doors, and around corners until we reached a huge, locked door. Rosemary explained that the main door to the chapel was on the other side, on the street. The villagers entered from that door, while Rosemary and her family entered from this interior door and sat in the balcony, which was accessible only from the castle. I was finally escorted to my room at three in the morning. This meant three hours of sleep, at best.

The next day, the prince monopolized me. He drove me through the woods to his hunting lodge bordering the Black Forest. We stopped at a brewery, where the manager and his wife helped select some special German phonograph records the prince wanted me to have. Rosemary seemed moody when we returned, so instead of going deer hunting with the prince, I stayed to help her prepare for the evening. It was bound to be another late one. She had also invited a young man from Frankfurt to spend the weekend while I was there, and the prince's secretary planned to join us too.

As we sat through another elaborate dinner, I felt awkward because the only English spoken was between Rosemary and me. Also, I felt as if I was getting more attention from her gentleman friend than she was. Try as I might to get an answer about when I could get a ride back to the train station, the topic kept changing every time I brought it up. No one would commit, and it was obvious they wanted me to stay on. I was beginning to feel as if I had been kidnapped. Finally, the prince agreed to drive me to Augsburg the next day, where I could get the train back to Munich.

We set out, but just before we reached Augsburg, the prince made me understand that I was in for another ordeal. He was taking me to visit his mother and sister. Woe is me! Soon, another castle loomed before me—the very one, I learned, that General George S. Patton had used to quarter his soldiers during World War II. Patton had allowed the castle's aristocratic owners to remain on the property and live in the servant's cottage. He saw that they had enough to eat and that the women were left unmolested, so the countess, Prince Fuggar's mother, had the highest regard for Patton; hence, for all Americans, so I was in her favor.

There was quite a crowd for lunch, and the countess insisted I stay for afternoon tea as well before I was chauffeured to the train. The prince was still reluctant to say a final farewell and insisted he come to Munich and bring a friend, suggesting I find a date for his friend. This I resolved not to do, but the prince arrived in Munich anyway. We had a leisurely dinner in an exclusive restaurant, and before the evening was over he was trying to convince me to stay until his wife returned (up to this point there had been no mention of her) so they could take me to the Salzburg Music Festival. I insisted that my itinerary would not allow for such a change in plans.

Once safely on the train coursing along the scenic Rhine, I began to collect my thoughts. My Irishman! Monsignor Doheny! My European adventures! The past, the present, the future! What was God really asking of me? Then, from the depths of my soul, came an interior voice: "Can any one man satisfy you when I alone dwell in the deepest recesses of your heart?" The message was seeping in just as surely as the waters flowed along the banks of the Rhine. My true longing was becoming clear. I would indeed have to resolve things when I returned home.

The last stop on our trip was the ancestral home of my Irishman, where I even kissed the Blarney Stone, hanging by my feet. As we sailed away, I watched the Emerald Isle disappear from view, thinking of the secret in my heart. I thought back to Rome, when the eight of us had tossed coins into the famous Trevi Fountain, which, according to legend, would guarantee our return. I realized that of all in our group, I was the least likely ever to come back. Both the Visitation Sisters and the Sisters of the Good Shepherd were semicloistered orders.

As our steamer neared home, passing into the Saint Lawrence River, I stood leaning over the rail, wondering how I would keep afloat for the next year. I had a year's teaching contract to fulfill, and at the end of the year, I intended to make my big announcement. As yet, I had not made my decision public, nor had I told my family.

We checked into a hotel, and the next morning I awoke early, walked down to the water, and dove into the Saint Lawrence for a pre-breakfast dip. As I plunged into the current, the force of the water took me by surprise and I felt the Saint Christopher medal forcibly ripped from my neck. I was stunned that my mother's gift to me was gone. It was as if the Saint had heeded my mother's words to take care of me while I was away, and then said, "I'm finished with her!" I had, no doubt, pushed Saint Christopher too far, and he considered his duty done. With the powerful current, there was no hope of retrieving the medal, and I struggled even to get myself back to shore, adding another near miss to the list I had already accumulated.

6

Answering the Call

Only in God is there security.
All else is shifting sands.

BACK IN SAINT LOUIS, I settled into my new job as a first grade teacher, counting on this brief means of livelihood to provide the dowry necessary for my entrance into the Good Shepherd Order. I soon realized what a challenging grade I had agreed to teach. I loved my little first graders, but it took me awhile to get them reading. The other first-grade teacher had her group mastering the skill within the first several months. It was not until the last few months that mine made a breakthrough, just in time to keep me from feeling like a failure. The mothers of these children were supportive, however. One, whose little son stuttered, thanked me for my patience. Her son's nervousness and speech problem had subsided and he was able to read. My elation stemmed from the fact that all the kids, who were dropouts from their previous first grades, seemed to blossom at once.

Christmas that year was difficult. My Irishman was on leave from the Marines and had come to visit. By then, I felt certain of where I was headed. I told him what the Monsignor had discerned, and said I had decided to enter a Convent. Since the Monsignor was his mentor, he had to accept the news. Two dates were all we had; there was no sense prolonging the agony. We had seriously considered the prospect of being together for life. It was hard enough to feel my own emotional tug at ending this sort of relationship, but to think of what it was doing to my Irishman made it even harder.

Soon after, I received a letter from the Good Shepherd Sisters in Chicago. The Monsignor had been at work already. The Superior from the Order announced that she was coming to Saint Louis for a few days and would like to meet me. Was this the answer I'd been waiting for?

I knew now that I had to tell my family, and it wasn't going to be easy. I told Mommy first because I thought she would be the happiest about my decision and the least shocked. She was not as enthusiastic as I'd hoped she would be, and she was concerned about the effect my decision might have on Daddy.

I decided to try my grandmother next, figuring she might be easier. After all, as a young woman she too had considered the same life for herself and probably would have gone through with it had her parents not been so adamantly against it. But in those days, marriage was arranged by the parents, and she was an obedient child. She did seem more sympathetic, but was concerned about the effect my decision would have on my grandfather. Of the two men I had to face, I figured my grandfather would probably be the hardest, so I saved him for last.

I bolstered myself and called Daddy at his office to ask if

I could take him out for lunch. This was not unusual, since I would sometimes meet my grandfather or father if I had gone downtown to shop and found myself near the Buder Building. What was unusual this time was that the luncheon was on me, so I think my father suspected something was up. I thought it would be wise to break the news in a public place, so his reaction would, out of necessity, be more constrained.

When we were seated and had ordered, I began. "Daddy, I have something important I want to tell you." He nodded. "I've waited for a long time now," I said, "and I believe God wants me for His spouse." Tears appeared in my father's eyes as he stammered, "Well, I expected you might be announcing your engagement, but I wasn't prepared for this!" It was hard enough to see a man cry, but causing this reaction in my own father was almost more than I could bear. We finished the rest of our lunch mostly in silence.

Now for my grandfather. Since he was eighty-two, he no longer went to the office regularly, so I picked him up at home and took him to one of his favorite restaurants. I began the conversation much as I had with Daddy. When I had finished, he gave no response at all. Afraid my words had fallen on deaf ears, I asked him, "Did you hear what I just said?"

"Just because I heard doesn't mean I understand," he said. He too had been expecting an announcement of marriage. I guess I had been hiding my secret all too well. Just to make further conversation, I told him the Convent was quite close to where he lived. He said he knew it well, and went on to describe the high cement wall that surrounded the building taking up an entire city block. He mentioned a parlor inside, where a poem he had written was hanging on the wall.

"Oh," I said, amazed and somewhat relieved, "then you know these Sisters and about the work they do trying to help girls who have been in trouble."

"Know them?" he exclaimed, "I used to visit them each year at Christmas and give a dollar to every girl under their care." I knew he was a very generous man, but this much involvement surprised me. And it was even directed by Catholics! I relaxed a bit then and told him, "The family can come to visit me once a month."

His face showed no emotion, but his words were adamant. "If you do this thing, don't ever expect to see me again." I couldn't believe what I had heard. I worried that what he was really saying was that my decision would hasten his death. It had been painful enough to give him the message, and now I felt almost as if I were being disowned, abandoned by my best friend. I went on to tell my brothers, one by one. Each was unbelieving, so didn't offer any encouragement either. I worried about all the agony I seemed to be causing—which depleted the initial joy of my decision.

The date I was to enter the Sisters of the Good Shepherd was set for October, and I still had the summer ahead of me. On a trip to Cincinnati, I visited the Good Shepherd Home and talked with the Superior to see if I picked up the same sense of devotion to their special vocation of caring for unfortunate girls as was true of the Sisters in St. Louis. What had helped to convince me about this Order was their fourth vow. Besides the vows of Poverty, Chastity, and Obedience, they also practiced a fourth vow of

Zeal—zeal for the salvation of souls. I took this to apply not only to the girls and women they nurtured, who were the socially and emotionally vulnerable, but to all who were in need of conversion. I definitely wanted my father and grandfather to embrace the Catholic faith so we could be fully united. These Sisters in Cincinnati seemed to possess a strong spirit of dedication in the attention they gave their charges, so I was satisfied I had made a good choice.

On the way back from Cincinnati, I joined my parents and brothers at Castle Park, Michigan, our old favorite resort. I knew it would probably be the last time we would enjoy it together. I certainly was not expecting a former suitor to turn up, someone I had never considered seriously as a mate. He explained that he was just passing through and thought he would look me up, but after a stroll on the beach, I discovered his appearance was hardly casual. He had followed us there with a purpose, surprising both me and my parents. I had no idea he still cared until we took a stroll on the beach, and I heard the passion in his voice. "I need you," he said. "Please, let us lie down here." His fervor and insistence alarmed me, and I found myself shaking. "Here, on the cold sand, without a blanket?" I managed to say. "It's getting chilly with the lake breeze coming up. I'd really rather head back."

Whether he saw this as a rejection or simply the result of my naiveté, I don't know, but he politely escorted me back, trying to convince me all the while that my entering the Convent was a mistake. He looked upon it as a waste and thought I would do far better to become someone's bride. He pleadingly put in a plug for himself. My "good night" at the door was firm, and I never saw him again. I did, however, later receive a letter from him after I had invited him to my First Profession as a Sister of the Good Shepherd.

Dear Sister Mary Madonna,

Though rather late I write this to convey to you my most sincere thanks for inviting me. Never before have I witnessed anything as dignified and impressive.

I must apologize for leaving without a chance to wish you the best, but the practice was calling [he was a doctor] *and I could not remain any longer. Perhaps, too, I was not quite up to it.*

You should know, however, that I have never seen a person appear so supremely happy. All this makes me more content— more content to know that you are doing what you know to be right for you; knowing that each day you will be doing more and more good and will, as a result, learn to love Him as much as is humanly possible.

I am aware that you have many people to remember in your prayers. I do ask that once in a while you may say a little one that I just simply have the strength to do what is right in this confusing world. You might also pay attention particularly to those young ladies we occasionally send you from Catholic Charities— the ones whom we fail to reach.

My most sincere thanks to you for the past and my special wishes for much joy and happiness in the future.

Ray

Just a month before my entering the Sisters of the Good Shepherd over Labor Day weekend, my oldest brother and I decided to drive to Colorado with another friend, a geology professor from Washington University. We thought it would be a lark to scale some of the Rockies around Estes Park. I especially wanted to try Longs Peak, one of the highest in the range at 14,259 feet. I had tried to scale it during college, but had had to turn back because of ominous weather. This time I was determined to make it to the summit.

Instead of striking out for Longs Peak immediately, we decided to ease in to it and scale the smaller Hallett Peak, elevation 12,713, first. Knowing no better, we tried the head-on frontal attack. Midway up, I noticed some discarded rope and a pick. I called this to my brother's attention, taking it as a clue that we needed something more than we had. Our bodies were our sole equipment. My brother shrugged it off and kept plowing ahead. I was close behind him when all of a sudden he disappeared around a rocky buttress. The rocky terrain at this height had very loose footing and, of course, I didn't have climbing boots, so I decided to wait there on the slope before going further. I called to my brother to let him know I was waiting, but got no answer. Our friend was trailing behind, and I yelled to him to go back down. He wasn't making any headway anyway, and I said I would join him. I didn't want to be responsible for two mishaps.

When I reached our friend, he was still breathless, apparently with a low tolerance for altitude, and was slumped by a creek. "Why were you two so far ahead of me?" he complained. "Couldn't you tell I was having trouble?" Then it dawned on him: Where was the third member of our party?

"My brother is the one you should be concerned about," I snapped. "We've got to sit here and pray him to safety!" With every word I uttered, I strained for sight of my brother. The more time that went by, the more restless my friend became, suggesting we should go for help before nightfall. I insisted that we keep praying until a given time, setting 3:30 p.m. as the outside limit.

At a quarter past three, I paused in my prayers. I heard something, and as I looked in the direction of the sound, I saw some activity way up above—a rock slide. I knew it had to be caused by something. Sure enough, a small figure, still upright, was barely visible. "It's him," I shouted, "but he's in a very precarious spot. I know. I was there. We've got to keep praying him down to safety." At this point, our friend's concern for my brother increased as his prayers became more earnest.

When my brother approached, he no longer had a jaunty air about him. Any edges of cynicism regarding his faith seemed to have been polished smooth. When I told him, "You were prayed down every inch of the way, I want you to know," he offered no rebuttal, only silence. Something had come over him. I was awed by God's protective guidance and supremely grateful to have my brother back, so whatever took place between God and my brother I did not question.

The next day we successfully scaled Hallett Peak but by a different approach. As I stood above the neighboring peaks capped with clouds, I wanted to stay forever. Had we been spared the previous day's trauma, perhaps this day's adventure to the top would have seemed less significant. But now, gazing on the expansiveness of this ocean of peaks and into the depths of the shadowed valleys below, I reflected that the life I was about to embrace would bring me low. I would, with measured steps, be led through humility's valleys before I reached the dizzying heights I aspired to. Could I really fully commit to pledge my heart to God forever?

* * *

These were the countdown days. Today was September 8, the Feast of the Nativity of the Blessed Virgin Mary. She had been my source of inspiration all along. Now, as I stood at a place that felt like Heaven's threshold, misty clouds surrounding me like puffs of incense, I felt her mantle wrapped around me. I was secure in the knowledge that she would lead me to her son, no matter how trying the journey. It took a yesterday to make a today. With these thoughts, I descended, knowing I must embrace Christ as my first and only love no matter the cost.

Longs Peak was our final challenge. I was so confident that we would make it that I decided to carry a sign to plant on top. I wanted something durable enough to withstand the elements, and I wanted the message to remain readable. I found an old board in the back of Bear Lodge where we spent the night, and was industriously using a hammer and nail to pound holes to form letters when my brother wandered up and asked, "You're not going to drag that up there, are you?"

"Of course," I said. "If we make it, this will too." Sensing he could not dissuade me, he left me hammering away. I finished the message: *Our Lady of the Summit, lead us to our Eternal Goal.* Carrying the sign, we set out. The rangers recommended just one trail up to the top and warned us to turn back if we hadn't made it beyond timberline by a certain time. Otherwise, we would not make it back down before nightfall. Even so, we'd have to hope that the weather would be in our favor, and no one could be sure of that in the mountains.

On this climb as well as the last one, our friend was soon

having the struggle of his life keeping pace with us. My brother was ahead of me, and I kept turning back to yell to the third member of our party to keep up. "If we can make it, so can you," I shouted. "Just keep moving!"

When I caught up with my brother before summiting, he reached down for the sign and said, "Here, let me take your trophy." I thought, how ironic that the former skeptic should carry the message. He scrambled forward. I was directly beneath him when a rock dislodged and came crashing down on my right foot. My big toe began to swell and throb. I was not wearing climbing boots, only loafers. I was afraid to remove my shoe lest I not be able to put it on again. The trek was only half over. We still had to descend.

We waited for our friend to catch up before we planted the sign, then started down directly, knowing it would take us longer now because of my injury. Going up takes endurance, but going down takes skill, even under ideal conditions. Now I had to really concentrate on my footing. We had no flashlights, so it was a race against nightfall. It was well after dark when we stumbled to the car, fatigued, famished, and thirsty. Our first thought was to find a restaurant. My foot could wait. After a deep sleep we awoke the next day in a state of delayed exultation. We had made it. God had been our guide once again.

Seven years later, a podiatrist removed the toenail from my big toe. All this time I had been living with a black fungus building up under the nail dating back to the injury. I simply accepted it as a memento of another close call. Up to this point, I could count seven: two auto incidents, two water incidents, at least three mountain incidents. I always relished hearing my grandfather recite the jingle, "One, two, three, four, five, six, seven! All good children go to Heaven!" But I wasn't ready for that. I had more living to do. None of these close encounters dampened my spirit of adventure. They simply instilled in me the necessity of remaining prepared to meet my Creator at any time.

Significantly enough, one thing I did before altering my life was to accept a role in *Death Takes a Holiday* by Alberto Casella—a play I had also tried out for back in college at Washington University, when I was taking drama as a second major. I was attracted to the symbolism and the relationship the play bore to my life even then. In this drama, a young woman, Grazia, is attracted to only one suitor. Death succeeds in courting her. For me, entering the convent would mean death to a world of allurements, attractions, and attachments. I would be won over, instead, by a life of sacrificial dedication. My mother also tried out for this play. She and I obtained the female leads. I was to be Grazia, she my mother! It was only a month until, in real life, my mother would relinquish me to the hand of my Creator on the Feast of Christ the King, October 25, 1953.

7

The Ultimate Sacrifice

Gratitude is humility of heart,
considering all as gifts.

WHEN MY DAY came to enter the Convent, Daddy was unable to take the strain of a final farewell and did not accompany me to the Convent. Our last interaction was a game of tennis. When we finished, I got into the car with my mother and brothers, and we drove away. I stood in the Convent parlor and said good-bye to them. I was wearing a black Postulant outfit, quite a contrast to the fashionable attire I had just discarded. I had on a black skirt and stockings, black blouse and cape, and a black net snood which constrained my long locks. Thirty years later, in an anniversary card my mother sent me, she wrote:

As your brothers and I left the Convent after escorting you there, a beautiful red sunset appeared in the sky. I shall always remember that. It symbolizes to me the peaceful joy of a life well chosen. I am most thankful to our Lord for choosing you as His own.

At last I realized my mother appreciated what I had chosen to do with my life!

Four other Postulants had arrived ahead of me, including one young girl from the Philippines, so I became the fifth in our little band. As Postulants, we were expected to retire early after evening recreation, instead of joining the Novices and the rest of the community in the chapel for Night Prayers. After a week had elapsed, I was growing tired of being treated like a baby and dismissed early for bed. Occasionally the other Postulants and I would think up some mischief. On one occasion, I obtained the cooperation of three of the Postulants and swore the fourth, a goody-goody, to secrecy. At the entrance to the bathroom, we placed a large pan used for dishwashing partially filled with water with a bar of soap afloat. An attached sign read *Footbath. Use before entry.* On one of the two bath stalls, we tied a large ribbon salvaged from a funeral bouquet, fixed in such a way as to impede use. A sign designated *Water rationed!* We locked the single toilet stall from inside and placed a sign on the door: *Don't use! I'm overworked!* By the time our pranks were discovered, we were lying in bed, with the covers pulled over our faces to smother our giggles.

When it was time for my family's first visit, Daddy came too, and they brought my dog, Winkie; but my grandfather was not present. This concerned me. One of my most fervent hopes was that he would accept my path and that, furthermore, he himself would convert to Catholicism. Before everybody left, I cuddled Winkie in my arms and posed for a picture in the garden. It was hard for me to separate from my family when the hour was up. Seeing the tears well up in Daddy's eyes made it even harder.

Four months went by, and still no visit from Grandfather. The number of Postulants was now down to two; three had left. Two of them apparently were not suited for this type of dedication. However, in the case of the little Filipina, it was a visa issue and I felt her loss. I became lonely and unsure of my own future, wondering what I was still doing here. The next step in my progress was the Clothing Ceremony, in which I would receive my habit and become a Novice, but I began to wonder whether I had made the wrong choice after all. Was I just too stubborn to leave?

The Provincial, the Sister who headed all the houses in the Saint Louis Province, knew by now how important it was for me to see my grandfather. I had bargained with God that if this was the life He had chosen for me, I needed a sign, the conversion of my grandfather before time ran out. One day the Provincial asked whether I'd like to go visit my grandfather, since he was not coming to visit me. I was amazed because we were cloistered and never left the grounds for anything but a doctor's appointment. I was given permission to go see my grandfather for two hours, but was not to let anyone know except my Novice Directress. I jumped at the opportunity.

My mother came to pick me up. When we got to my grandfather's, he was lying on the divan in his robe. As soon as he saw me in my black outfit, he said, "Maria, come sit beside me." Strange, I thought, since my middle name was Marie, not Maria, and no one ever used my middle name. My grandmother had made my favorite treats—vanilla wafers and orange ice—but before we helped ourselves, she said, "Grandfather has something to say." He looked at me with a sheepish schoolboy side glance, made the sign of the cross, and said the words of blessing over our refreshments, revealing an acceptance of the Catholic faith. I could hardly restrain my tears. What further sign of approval did I need from the Lord? "I came to see you," I told my grandfather as I left. "Now you must come to see me."

My family came for another visit, but still no grandfather. I knew time was running short, both for him and for me. He was growing weaker. How much longer could he hold out beyond his eighty-three years? The next month would mark the sixth month of my Postulancy, the time when I should be receiving the habit to become a Novice. I had already put it off for two months. I needed an answer to my plea for my grandfather's conversion. On March 25, the Feast of the Annunciation, which commemorates the submission of the Virgin Mary to the Holy Spirit when asked to become the Mother of the Messiah, I spent all day in prayer on my knees in front of the Blessed Sacrament in the chapel. Was this way of life really God's will for me? Would He see to my grandfather's conversion?

The next day, the Sister in charge of the Novices came and asked me to follow her. "There is someone I think you'd like to see," she said. It wasn't a visiting day, but when she swung open the door to the parlor, I saw a familiar balding, gray head. Yes, my mother had come, and brought my grandfather. Too weak to rise from the chair, he reached out his hand and said, "Don't let them take me away. I want to stay here with you. They can lay straw on the floor for me to sleep here to be with you."

This was my signal.

"If you want to be with me," I said, "then you'll want to become a child of God just like me, my brothers, Mommy, and my grandmother, won't you?"

His simple reply was, "I want to be whatever you are."

When the Priest arrived to hear the Nuns' confessions, he was escorted into the parlor. I explained, "Father, my grandfather would like to become a child of God." I didn't want to use the word *baptize* in front of my grandfather, lest it scare him off. The Priest obligingly took my grandfather's hand and asked, "Are you sorry, Mr. Buder, for anything you have done wrong in your life?"

"Oh, yes," my grandfather responded in a childlike manner. "I never wanted to hurt anybody."

With this, the Priest took the cup of water presented him by the Sister who had brought him into the parlor, made the sign of the cross on my grandfather's forehead, and said, "With this water I baptize you a child of God, Mr. Buder, in the name of the Father, Son, and Holy Spirit."

My grandfather seemed at peace when he was led from the parlor. I wondered if I would ever see him again. The next day he had to be taken to the hospital. There he received the Sacrament of the sick, and one week later, he passed away at the age of eighty-three.

Ten days later, I entered into retreat in preparation for my Clothing Ceremony. Still I struggled with doubts. Was I really ready to labor selflessly in my Order for the errant young women whom the Good Shepherd had led to His fold? It was one thing to adapt to communal living, to accept celibacy, to deny oneself the ordinary pleasures, comforts, and conveniences of life, but quite another to spend long hours of surveillance over brooding, cantankerous young women. I had been sheltered from life's sordidness. Now I would be brought face to face with its victims.

Would my years of enjoying life's finer conditions make me unfit to serve these girls? Would they accept me, coming from a background so different from their own? There was no sense in torturing myself further with these thoughts. The only way to see if I could do it was to jump in. After all, becoming a Novice was only the first step in the five-year sequence of preparation to becoming a fully professed Sister.

Having my long hair cut in order to receive the veil was a trauma all its own. I felt like a lamb shorn of its fleece. Kneeling in the middle of the aisle with head bowed, wearing the white habit and veil of the Novice I waited in suspense for my new name to be bestowed. When I heard the name Sister Mary Madonna, my heart leaped for joy. I had so wanted a title of Blessed Mother Mary.

At the reception for friends and family in the parlor, my favorite cake was served—devil's food, of all things, decked with white icing. By the end of the day, I realized how blessed I was and how many proofs of God's love I had received. Now it was up to me to respond as a faithful daughter, a loving spouse. I would try not to look upon anything He asked as being too difficult.

For a time, I was the only Novice in the Novitiate, and one of my duties was to wash the dishes after the main meal. As I was lifting a stack of thick stoneware dinner plates, I couldn't raise them high enough to clear the edge of the counter. They clattered onto the brick floor with a racket that could have raised the dead. It was customary to make amends for such carelessness by wearing a piece of the broken object strung around the neck when making the rounds in the refectory acknowledging the fault before each Sister on your knees. I had enough pieces to choke me! I was mortified and during the next family visit, confided to my parents what I had done. Instead of reproaching me as I expected, Daddy blurted, more seriously than facetiously, "Good! Now maybe they'll send you home!"

When I began my job assisting with the younger girls, I heard the word *incest* for the first time. I must have looked rather blank, because Sister took it upon herself to explain the word to me right then. A number of the children we were working with had been victims of this crime. These girls needed individual attention, and some acted inappropriately in order to get it. Negative attention relieved their guilt and was certainly better than no attention at all, so it was necessary for us as adults not to be drawn into this trap. I soon realized I needed to treat them with firmness, patience, caring, and consistency, to provide the stability they so badly needed.

When three years had elapsed, it was time to make my First Profession of commitment to the Community and to receive the silver heart and the black veil. I sent my Irishman an invitation to the ceremony, but he declined, writing instead:

> My absence will demonstrate more than my presence. This occasion requires of so many, and particularly your loving family, to make handmaids of Joy and Sorrow.

I could not have said it better myself, for the sacrificial element was becoming more evident as my service continued.

Soon added to my duties was the job of elementary principal. I was already required to teach some of the classes, including English, ethics, and physical education. Then it was decided to merge the younger class with the older girls. I was exhausted. I had no time for recreation, no time for myself, and no time for scheduled prayer with the community. It nearly crushed my spirit never to get outside, especially on those beautiful, bright, crisp fall days, which kept my soul alive, It interfered with my love of nature and my need for contemplation.

As the time for my final vows neared, I was taken by surprise when I was asked whether I might like to spend some preparation time at our Mother House in Angers, France. I had taken French in high school and college, so was somewhat familiar with the language. Besides, my mother had been schooled in her ancestral tongue and spoke French fluently. She had always wanted to visit the home of her grandparents, and now I was her excuse. Daddy agreed to go with her as well. What a delightful twist my entering a cloistered order had taken. Off to globetrotting!

Once again, I was on my way to Europe, along with five others from my Order. Our group of darkly-clad figures—we wore black for traveling—escorted by my parents, caught the attention of those aboard the Cunard liner. Several priests became friendly and dubbed my father "The Chap," short for *chaplain*. He enjoyed the compliment.

We arrived on August 15, and our final vows were set for December 8. In the Angers community, I soon became known as *La Grande Soeur*. The French, as a rule, were short, so my tall, willowy, white-gowned figure attracted attention, especially when I was on the floor of the refectory with brush, bucket, and burlap, scrubbing away at the stone tiles.

I felt comfortable in the French setting, but the reality of the upcoming final commitment began to throw me into a panic. I would have to take a vow, not for just a year this time, but "for life." As I struggled with this uncertainty, my body was wracked with sobs at night. One morning, as the day grew closer to final vows, I awoke with swollen eyes from a night of crying. I sought the English-speaking Assistant. On my knees at her side, I revealed my plight. In motherly fashion, she leaned over and let me sob on her shoulder. I was consoled by her advice—namely, that God would be true to His promises to me. This thought reversal helped me to gain my equilibrium.

On December 8, I pronounced my final vows in the historic Saint Nicholas Abbey on the grounds of the Mother House in Angers. I was ready now to return to the United States as a fully professed Sister of the Good Shepherd.

I later learned that while I was in France taking my final vows, Tom Dooley, a former suitor, had passed away. By then he had become a famous humanitarian, establishing medical clinics and hospitals in Laos. He also had written several books, including *The Night They Burned the Mountain*, *The Edge of Tomorrow* and *Deliver Us From Evil*. Sadly, during his time in Southeast Asia, he had been stricken with malignant melanoma. He died at the young age of thirty-four.

Even though I had considered him a *beau gallant* while we were dating, I noticed a new depth of character when he set out to be of service as a medic in foreign danger zones. I had really wanted the chance to meet him again in Saint Louis after his mission. When I realized how much he had done in his short life, he became one of my heroes. I like to think of him as a Christ figure who burned brightly like a comet arcing through the sky. Through the zeal of his short life span, his mission was complete.

8

On the Move

I sometimes get lost in order to be found.

I TOOK UP my duties with our Order in Saint Louis, which included teaching some high school classes as well as being Group Mother. Formerly, the girls had lived in one large dorm; but now they were divided into smaller groups, with a Sister acting as head of each group. The girls in my group called me Mother Madonna. Just eight months later, I was a little puzzled when the Provincial said she would like me to move to Kansas City to be Directress for the girls. "The house there seems jinxed," she told me. "We may have to close it in a few years." Well, if that was the case, at least I knew I wouldn't be trapped there forever.

Once in Kansas City, I found myself responsible for everything—from supervising the cook to directing the choir, though I did not play either the organ or the piano. I taught, served as school Principal, and handled the ordering of supplies as well as being a Group Mother. I was also responsible for family communications. When the girls weren't the problem, the parents were. To this day, I don't know how I made it through the first week. But I persevered, and once the girls saw that I had their interests at heart, they began to rise to my expectations.

Soon I was called back to Saint Louis with the news that my maternal grandmother had slipped into a coma. I was with her when she died. When I got back to Kansas City, I had another death to contend with: It was clear that our Order's work there was dying out, and we would have to close the home.

In the next two years, I moved from city to city. It was like joining the Army and seeing the world. I was next sent to Phoenix, to be in charge of one of the cottages on the campus of our Order's institution there. My first impression of the Southwest was of openness—no walls, no fences, walks lined with date palms and citrus trees around the white stucco cottages of the girls. This wasn't going to be hard to take. But the assignment was not as rosy as were the premises.

I got along well with the girls and the lay staff, so well that my popularity seemed to cause a certain discomfort among the powers-that-be. At first I had to play the dual role of parent and teacher, in the classroom part-time and then serving as a housemother in the girls' cottage. It was difficult dismissing the girls from the class I taught and then being in the cottage to welcome them "home" immediately afterward. However, the girls were soon performing well, and I could even leave for the weekend and know that they'd keep working while I was gone. Soon, however, for reasons of economy, a lay couple was hired to take my place as cottage parent, while I was retained to teach full time. The girls demonstrated their resentment that I'd been removed as cottage parent by throwing things out of their bedroom windows on the first night of my absence. As you can imagine this did not go over well with the new cottage parents assigned.

The Order had a lodge in Prescott, Arizona, the mile-high town, for the girls and the Sisters. It was always a welcome relief to go there and leave the conflicts and the oven that was Phoenix. I loved to hike and relished the moments of adventurous solitude in nature, which always brought me close to my Creator.

In my free time I wandered the woods and sometimes got lost, but fortunately found my way back—though on at least one occasion I wasn't so sure that I'd make it in one piece. I was in the habit of climbing up to a rocky perch to meditate, clothed in my black ankle-length habit. One day as I was making my way toward my prayer rock, I heard little whimpers which attracted my attention. I saw three little whelps hiding in a hole at the foot of the rock. Shortly afterwards I heard baying in the woods. Before I knew it, three scrawny dogs were glaring up at me from below, one in the middle and the other two on each side. "Oh God," I thought, "this is the old warrior-surrounding technique. Please inspire in me what to do."

The only direction left for me to go was back deeper into the woods, to avoid their jaws. Fortunately, I found a trail heading in the direction of our cabin, but I could feel the dogs closing in on me. I kept walking at an even, determined pace until I could almost hear their heavy breathing behind me. Then I invented a surprise tactic. I stopped suddenly, pivoted in place, which caused my long black skirt to whip around, and glared back at them. This gesture took them by surprise and they backed away, so I again wheeled around as I continued my procession. After several more of these maneuvers, I was actually in sight of the lodge. As soon as the dogs caught wind of civilization, they gave up the chase. One more incident where God came to the rescue!

A swim suit had been one of the first things I'd been given when I arrived in Phoenix. I couldn't believe that Pope John XXIII had relaxed the rules to this extent, but the Superior informed me it was therapy for arthritic Sisters to use our small kidney-bean enclosed pool. I had specifically relinquished swimming upon entering the Order. But when the Superior took a group of Sisters to Ensenada, Mexico, where our vacation spot faced the Pacific, I thought, why not "baptize" the suit?

I leaped into the ocean with abandon, not considering that I hadn't been swimming in twelve years, that a recent bout of flu had left my ribs sore from coughing, and that the Pacific waters were unfamiliar to me but also quite cold. The chill was a shock, but what was more of a shock was how far I quickly drifted after only a few sidestrokes. When I tried to lift my arm and signal distress, the little Spanish Sister who had accompanied me to the shore just waved back. I figured I better swim for all I was worth, but this only tired me out, plus I made no headway. I could see the Superior up on the cliff now, looking down. Surely she could see what was happening—but she turned and walked away.

I began to pray, "Please Lord, don't let me panic. If you want me now, it's because you know I am ready." Then a calm came over me. I realized there was no use struggling. I could see I had drifted so far that I couldn't see the Sister on the shore any more, but I also could see that the current had shifted and was now washing me toward land on an angle. The next problem was to avoid being sucked against the reefs, and there were many.

By the time I came up on the beach, my hands and feet were cut and bleeding. I could barely walk on the rocky shore to rejoin the other Sister. I could scarcely talk when asking for a towel. It was twenty minutes before I quit shivering long enough to walk back to the house. I didn't even attempt to explain what had happened. I just jumped into a hot shower.

The Grand Canyon beckoned when the Superior decided to take a group of us, traveling all the way there and back in one day. After a five-hour road trip, I couldn't wait to hop out and explore. To my dismay, we were told we had only ten minutes for sightseeing before assembling for lunch at Bright Angel Lodge on the rim of the canyon.

I had no interest in eating when there was all this beauty to drink in. My first glimpse into the sheer drop-off of the canyon was a peak experience. I had to catch my breath! The sensation was of being drawn into the eternal embrace. I wanted to stay and be lost in it; the agelessness of this chasm made me wonder what eternity was like. Unfortunately, I was ushered to rejoin the group.

But the Superior later surprised us with another trip to the Grand Canyon that included two overnights in some cabins there. This second time, we arrived in time for dinner. The next morning we were given three hours free time, before we had to meet at the lodge for lunch at noon. How was I going to make it to Indian Garden, which lay 4.6 miles down the Bright Angel Trail, and back in that amount of time? There was but one thing to do, and that was to strike out at breakneck speed. I decided to see how far down I could go in one hour, calculating that it would take at least twice that time to hike back up.

It was a scorcher of a day. I tucked up my long skirts and tore down the trail, whipping past mule trains as the guides did a double take. My black skirts flapped around my ankles, startling the animals as well as the people on them. Even a few sturdy foreigners on their way up the trail warned me to slow down or I'd never have enough steam to reach the top again. They obviously were having a tough time of it themselves. I barreled on, stopping only briefly to take a photo or two.

After an hour, I still hadn't reached Indian Garden, but I was close enough to stand on an overlook and photograph it. I headed back up, retracing my steps with the same accelerated drive. Again I passed mule trains and hikers who had a hard time believing what they saw. Where was I getting this energy? Did I have concealed wings?

With just an hour left, I overtook a young Frenchman who bemoaned the fact that he was never going to make it up in time to catch his tour bus, which was leaving at noon for the next state. This was the same time I was supposed to meet the other Sisters. "We've got to at least try!" I told him. "I'm going to; and if I can, you can." This was challenge enough. Together, we reached the top at noon on the nose. My face was beet red. An older Sister urged me to sit down before I collapsed. I told her I actually felt fine and we had better join the other Sisters quickly.

By the end of lunch, though, I was feeling the aftereffects. Every muscle ached and my hip joints caught each time I took a step, to say nothing of the tightness in my calves, thighs, and hamstrings. The next morning, the Superior told me she had a plan to save me from myself. She had booked me on a mule train so that I could get down to Indian Garden. I had sized up the mules the day before and decided I was far better off afoot than astride. But I didn't complain, and gamely tried to figure out how to deal with the hard saddle and my long skirts without revealing too much leg when astride. The trip was well worth it, even if for several days after, I snapped, crackled, and popped with each move.

I took my camera wherever I went, and after the Grand Canyon trips, my collection of photographs became the basis for one of my first audiovisual programs, "The Story of Creation," which I used for the religious instruction of our girls back in Phoenix. In addition to my full-time teaching, I had been asked to go on closed-circuit TV for a half hour each morning so the girls could receive religious instruction in their cottages before going to school. I really enjoyed putting together these programs, but was suddenly directed to stop. Instead, I was told I needed to complete my credential as an English teacher so that a full salary could be requested from the state.

Before I knew it, I was going to Arizona State University full time to complete my degree in English, the subject I was already teaching, but the teachers needed accreditation. At first I missed not being involved with the girls anymore. Then I had to come to grips with my own need to be needed. It occurred to me that we Sisters often contrived to make our girls dependent on us, which ended up serving our needs rather than theirs. I examined myself intensely on this front, and this caused me to take a critical look at how our institutions were being run. Accepting money from the state made us compliant to secular norms. We were required to employ a ratio of secular employees, yet some of the Sisters who remained as cottage parents were protective of their own groups. This possessiveness created friction between the groups. Even some of the secular cottage parents got caught up in the tensions. What a subtle form of ego-feeding our "doing good" could be!

There was also infighting due to a state-funded program launched in the school. When one program was discontinued and its director ousted, I was given an ultimatum not to speak to the director on the outs. Now I was torn between Obedience and Charity. With guidance, I concluded that Charity should win out. As the conflicts grew, I figured the only way to complete my degree and get some peace was to reside elsewhere. I was granted permission to move in with another Order of Sisters who lived closer to Arizona State University.

My black-robed figure soon became a familiar sight on the ASU campus and stood out amidst those more scantily clothed due to style and the Arizona heat. I was taking sixteen hours per semester and working toward two degrees as well as the English credential. I had earned my Master of Education in 1968. With only thirty more credit hours, I could receive a Master of Counseling degree. I was also trying for a master's in Audio Visual Education since I already had taken some of the preliminary courses. But the departments clashed over the question of whether both degrees could be conferred at once. Two credits shy of a master's in Audio Visual Education, I obtained my Master of Counseling in June 1969.

This completed my reason for living outside our own Convent. I had spent five productive years altogether in Phoenix. With three degrees in hand, I knew it was time to move on.

*   *   *

My next stop was an assignment to San Francisco. Here I was asked to draw up a proposal for a transition home on the premises, which I ran for the girls who were leaving the nuns to go back into society, some to their own families, others to foster care or the equivalent. The plan I devised was designed to give these girls more privileges and outings than the ones who were in the more confined cottages. It was a way to ease the girls back into the mainstream. But once these freedoms were observed by the other girls and cottage attendants, resentment began to build, so I became a target. I felt the only way to save myself was to ask for a transfer, something not usually done nor taken lightly by the Superior. It was a risk and I knew it, but it was the only chance I had to retain my sanity in such a situation.

Eight months later, I was assigned to New Orleans. This was the first time since I had taken my vows that I actually had some free time to spend with the Sisters at recreation after dinner. Before, I always had been employed with the girls on a round-the-clock basis. By this time, our Rule permitted Sisters to watch TV for an hour a day. Though I didn't choose to watch television, I welcomed the free time. It wasn't long, though, before I learned that the house in New Orleans would also have to close its doors. Out of the four places I had been assigned, Kansas City, Phoenix, and San Francisco had been shut down. Soon I got word that the house in Tulsa, Oklahoma, would also have to close its doors.

In the midst of all this upheaval, I was given the opportunity to go to New Rochelle, New York, to attend Institute '70, an eight-week updating and renewal program run by the New York Diocese. It was very liberating to meet Sisters from many different Orders who were attempting to adapt to ever-changing societal norms, and I formed some lovely friendships. I learned a lot about the other programs in the different Provinces, and had a chance to share some of what I had been doing and what my dreams for the future were. It renewed a feeling of appreciation regarding our Order's possibilities.

After this session was over, I was invited to stay in New York City to help set up a new program run by the Good Shepherd Sisters called Project Outreach. This meant traveling on subways to Harlem and other areas to interview families or relatives of some of the girls in our program. Going from the openness of the West to this noisy, congested area of Manhattan directly across from Beth Israel Hospital, with sirens going round the clock and Dumpsters unloading in the early morning hours, was a shock. But it was short-lived. After nine months, I was sent to Denver to await word about a new assignment.

On the plane heading for Colorado, I tried to assess where I was. Here I was, forty-one years old, and in the past two years I had been moved four times. That kind of jostling is unsettling, to say the least. Not only did I have to meet new people each place I went, but I had to adjust to cultural differences. From the West, I dipped to the South. From the South, I had gone East. Now I was flying West, ultimate destination unknown.

What seemed particularly ironic was that I had joined a semicloistered Order where I would feel grounded. But where were my roots? To whom did I belong? Then, in the stillness of my heart, I drew strength from this message: "You belong to me. That is all that really matters. Let me do with you as I please." I knew that if I were able to believe this, to really let go and let God, I could never be a failure.

Soon I learned that my next assignment would be to Spokane, Washington, and I was off again. On the flight there, I began talking with a Priest who was coming home from giving a retreat in Denver. By the time we landed, he was eager to enlist my help for a retreat at Immaculate Heart Retreat Center in Spokane. It was there that I was soon introduced to the Charismatic movement. Never before had I been in an environment where people gathered to spontaneously break into song and prayer. Some of the prayer was even in an unidentifiable language, known to those familiar with the phenomenon as "speaking in tongues." When this went on, it was considered a joyful sign by the prayer community that the Spirit was at work in that person or group. I soon began attending such prayer meetings regularly.

But my Charismatic practice, along with the fact that I was still in my habit whereas the younger set was in lay clothing, put me out of step with my new community, which added to my stress. I had been asked to pioneer a short-term program for the girls in residential care in Spokane, which required long days of counseling and meeting with families. Sometimes the work was satisfying, when I could see families improve and, in some cases, be restored. But, often, by evening I was drained by the problems I had carried in my heart all day. I frequently ate dinner alone and in tears. Having noticed my condition, the Superior suddenly told me to discontinue this work for fear I was on the verge of a breakdown. Having had too much to do, I now had too little. What was it the Lord was asking of me at this juncture?

Not long thereafter, one of the Sisters observed my interest in photography and suggested, "Why don't you do something with that?" I began working on a slide presentation called "From Sea to Shining Sea," which contained photographs from eight different states; as well as another program, "The Cosmos in Christ," using quotes from Teilhard de Chardin and Saint Paul.

By summer I had been completely relieved of my responsibility as director of the short-term program for the girls. This left me free to attend a six-week House of Prayer experience in Pecos, New Mexico, at the Benedictine Abbey. In this environment we each received a counselor. Mine was none other than the Abbot himself, who asked whether I had ever thought of changing my apostolate—my chosen work of caring for these kinds of girls, for whom our Order had been founded.

Shortly afterwards I was introduced to Eurythmy, a form of liturgical dance best described as "visible speech." I was totally refreshed by this prayer form of using gestures to worship, and felt the weight on my shoulders lift. I also received notice of my official transfer to the Saint Paul Province, which I had requested. The house in Spokane to which I had relocated belonged to this Province. My "new beginning" was finally coming together. When I returned to Spokane, I expanded my audiovisual programs, learned how to use a two-projector dissolve system, and presented a budget on which to operate. I named my project the Media Ministry, and my first presentation was at a prison over on the eastern side of Washington.

It occurred to me that I could introduce body movement into some of my programs, especially with the use of the Eurythmy techniques I had learned at Pecos. I thought about the idea for three years before I got the courage to try it. In the meantime, I took lessons in modern dance from an Argentinian dancer in Spokane. She was so sincerely impressed when I interpreted the Lord's Prayer that it gave me the encouragement to include body movement in a sight/sound/prayer experience I was preparing for the Religious Education Congress in Seattle in the fall of 1975. I gave four presentations, and when the last one concluded, the audience was on its feet. It was made up of a real cross section—young adults, middle-aged and retired people, Sisters in the conservative habit and those without, lay people and a smattering of Priests. I did the body movements myself, and then invited the audience to try. Afterwards, a few folks told me what a freeing experience it had been. This helped to convince me I was on the right track.

It was a period of great creativity for me. I adapted my nature slides to *The Lord's Prayer*, a program that was televised each evening as the closeout for a television station in Spokane. I designed "From Sea to Shining Sea," with photographs I had taken across America, accompanied by patriotic music and a stirring narrative, just in time for the Bicentennial in 1976. In Spokane, the commissioner of the Bicentennial gave my program the official seal as one available for the celebration. I had seventy-five requests to show it. After one viewing, a man came up with tears in his eyes and said, "Sister, you not only sparked my patriotism, but you touched my soul."

"Oh, thank you, Lord," I said silently. This was the confirmation I had been waiting for. At last I felt I had formed a valid ministry.

Now I could see the reason for my many moves. I had been cast to the four winds of the United States, but always with a camera in my hand. The following year I added a program inspired by the book *Jonathan Livingston Seagull* by Richard Bach. I had collected photographs of seagulls from every vantage point, and put them together to create *The Gospel According to Jonathan*. The program, with themes of life, death, and resurrection, left viewers free to interpret the images, music, and words according to their personal leanings. For me, God was revealing Himself through it all, aided by the use of modern technology.

9

Running Toward God

If I don't use the gifts God has given,
I am not honoring my Creator.

NOT LONG AFTER I took up running, I got the idea of doing a marathon. Trying that at the age of fifty-plus might be quite an undertaking I knew. But I set my sights on the Boston Marathon and began training relentlessly, increasing my distance little by little in the attempt to qualify. In those days, the qualifying time for women forty and over was three hours and thirty minutes. I was already twelve years beyond the age of forty.

If I managed to succeed, I planned to collect contributions for those with multiple sclerosis, holding them in my prayers as I ran. Too little was known about this disease that ravaged so many, a great percentage in the Northwest, where I live. I contacted the local chapter in Spokane, and they were very enthusiastic. They made up flyers with my picture on them, and I passed them around to obtain pledges. Looking back, the fund-raising was the easier part of my race preparations.

One day when I was trying to increase my distance to twenty miles and faltered at mile thirteen, I began complaining to the Lord and I received a clear message. "You may feel that you are only shuffling. But many of the people you are running for can't even walk." Suddenly I realized that I at least had healthy limbs, even if those limbs felt like strangers at the moment. So I asked the Lord to take my discomfort then and there and transfer some strength to those suffering with MS. From then on, my pain seemed to disappear. I kept going, working my way up to twenty-six miles.

I was now ready to try a qualifying event for the Boston Marathon. The race I chose was next door in Coeur d'Alene, Idaho. I edged my way to the finish line with a time of 3:29:16—only 44 seconds to spare. I had qualified—but barely! In that year of 1982, at the age of fifty-two, I was probably one of the oldest women ever to do so. More than likely I was also the first Catholic nun.

But would I be going too far afield by actually competing in the Boston Marathon? I sought the advice of the Bishop. Having taken vows of Chastity, Poverty, and Obedience, I confessed that Obedience can be the hardest when it means stifling a God-given talent. I told him about qualifying to run the Boston Marathon and said that I wanted to do it for the cause of multiple sclerosis. The session ended with his blessing. "Sister," he said, "I wish some of my Priests would do what you are doing."

On April 18, 1982, I entered the Boston Marathon wearing a T-shirt the nuns had given me, with a paraphrase of a quote from Saint Paul (Phil. 3:4): "Running Toward the Goal." I approached the race like a neophyte. I left the house where I was staying in Framingham at 6:00 a.m., having breakfasted on just one banana, a glass of milk, and a granola bar. Before the race began at noon I was conscious of being hungry already. Also, I didn't drink water during the race, because I didn't want to take time for pit stops.

It took six minutes just to get to the starting line after taking off with more than six thousand runners. The first part of the race went pretty well, but during the last four miles there was such a temptation to break stride, I had to call on Jesus to help me continue running. For the final two miles, the crowds moved in on us so that it was suffocating and left scarcely any room for runners to pass each other. During the last stretch, my legs felt like lead, but I finished regardless with a time of 3:38:00.

My faith had pulled me through, and I crossed the finish secure in the belief that I was pleasing the very source of my creation. Having raised four thousand dollars in pledges for multiple sclerosis, I vowed to return the next year and do it again. I did, and managed to shave about six minutes off my time. By then I had learned to eat and drink a little more than practically nothing to get through twenty-six miles!

Part of the joy I found when I first started running was the chance to get out in nature. To this day, my problems seem to shrink when surrounded by God's Creation. Early on, I realized that whenever running became a bit monotonous I could focus on something along the route—a tree, a sunset, a flower—and compose a little verse about it. Haiku, three-line poems containing five, seven, and five syllables respectively, worked perfectly for this. Since I didn't carry paper, I just kept repeating the lines until I got home to write them down. It worked my brain while my body cruised on automatic. I came home with lines like these running through my head:

Sound of drip drip drip
Thawing echoes of winter
Harbingers of spring.

Over time I composed a number of these, repeating the lines to keep my rhythm going.

Caught up in the scene
Yellow, white, embraced by green
Lost in the daisies.

Songs of birds waking
Introducing a new day
Sweetly soothe the soul.

Stillness, then movement
Sudden breeze comes from nowhere
Stirring emotions.

On longer workouts, I recited the Rosary. Anything or anyone I prayed for helped me lose track of the miles and focus on the object of my prayers. Running not only helped me solve problems, it reduced my anxiety about them. It cleared my soul and took away any brooding darkness. To this day, when I am out running in nature, all worries seem trivial compared to the marvels that surround me. When you are out there alone on the roads, you know whose hands you are in.

A triathlon seemed a natural next step. After I returned from my first Boston Marathon, I noticed in the local paper an event called Troika—Greek for "three." This race required not only running 13.1 miles, but swimming 1.2 miles and bicycling 56 as well. At the time, I had only been introduced to running, and I knew how much it took to run a marathon and how depleted I felt after rushing through 26.2 miles at a goodly pace. At first, I couldn't imagine attaching a run to the end of a bike race, which in turn followed a swim. I also could not conceive of myself in a crowd of swimmers, being enmeshed in flailing arms and legs as we all started out at once. I was a novice at bike handling and just getting used to the machinations of a 10-speed. But the idea started to take hold.

I thought, "Well, I've done the epitome of foolishness by engaging in the marathon at my age, so what the heck, why not try this too?" I used to swim as a kid in Lake Michigan during our family summer vacations, and I rode my mother's balloon-tired bike as a child without any problem, so maybe, just maybe, I could do a triathlon. This was a relatively new sport at the time and was rapidly becoming popular. There were various distances attached to different events—including the toughest of all, the Ironman triathlons, which featured a 2.4-mile swim, a 112-mile bike race, and a full marathon of 26.2 miles. Whew! Tackling one of these was definitely a step up from running.

Whatever I did, living in the Northwest as I do, training presented some challenges during the winter months. Even by late fall, Spokane's weather made it hard to train outdoors, which is the only way I wanted to do it. This meant a four-month layoff from biking, and only minimal running. But I did what I could. Even in subzero temperatures, I would run through my neighborhood if the snow banks weren't too high. Otherwise, I kept toned with snowshoeing and cross-country skiing, and I could always swim at an indoor pool.

When the temperature dropped to twenty-two below zero one winter, people were staying in, afraid to breathe the freezing air. "You'll freeze your lungs," they told me, but I instinctively knew that if I was able to get my circulation going I'd get beyond the frozen point. I put a scarf over my nose and mouth. By the time I got home I was actually sweating. I looked like the abominable snowman, my eyelashes, eyebrows, and clothing decorated with ice particles. I learned to adapt as I persevered. But some dreary days in winter, I chose to hibernate, like many of God's other creatures. Except for swimming, I'd just take it easy, not fighting it. I'd just go with the flow of the season.

My first triathlon was a local event in Spokane called Heels & Wheels. The ¾-mile swim actually started in a pool. The 12-mile bicycle course was challenging, riddled with hills, and when I got off the bike to start the 10K run I felt like a drunken sailor. I couldn't even feel my legs, but somehow knew I was wobbling forward. When I caught up with the first person in front of me, I said to myself, "Well, I must be running after all even though I didn't feel my legs turning over."

The second triathlon I tried was the Troika, a Half Ironman of 1.2-mile swim, 56-mile bike, 13.1-mile run. In this race, I was still so new on the bike that after traveling twenty-five miles against headwinds, I was just five miles short of the finish line before I realized, "Hey, going against wind is like going uphill! Why don't you just shift down to make it easier?" Until then I had been pumping in the highest gear the whole time. When I got to the finish of the bike segment, I could hardly dismount. The volunteers had to work on me for thirteen minutes before my legs were ready to go out on the run. As usual, I learned by raw experience. But once again, when I finished, I wanted more.

As it turned out, the triple sports contained in the triathlon helped preserve me. I had reached a point of burnout with running events, so combining swimming, biking, and running in such an intense way rescued me from the continuous pounding of running. Though my running time dwindled, I was preserved from the lopsided intensity of endless running.

By now, I had discovered I was quite competitive and quite good. But I also found that my new interest carried some challenges I hadn't expected. Ultimately, I learned that I must be true to my own pace. I might outrun some people, even younger than I, but also allow others to outrun me. To preserve my own gifts, I had to be careful not to push beyond my capacity, or I would do myself in. When I was peaking during my tenth year of running, I learned there was such a thing as an addicted runner. Yet not to push at all left no room for improvement. This was the delicate balance. "Know thyself" and "To thine ownself be true," as the sayings go.

Of course, there were lots of decisions to make along the way—the proper clothing, for instance. Rather than stand out in a crowd, I decided to blend in with the rest of the scenery and wear what the rest of the triathletes wore—barring bikinis, of course. At first I was squeamish about wearing close-fitting tights, but eventually I got used to it because they were becoming quite common. If you're going to do what others do, you dress as they dress. Some people are surprised to see me in running clothes, but I stand out less that way. When I compete, I look just like another competitor, except perhaps for the cross on my necklace. Now I notice many other athletes, even Olympians, wearing the same.

Nonetheless, once I began running marathons and doing triathlon events, I seemed to have taken things beyond what some considered fitting activities for a Catholic nun. I began running about eight years after the running craze had begun, and there was another Sister in my Convent who had taken up running as well, but not to the extent that I had. She ran the Bloomsday race with me the first time I did it. That seemed acceptable. But after I tackled the Boston Marathon and moved on to triathlons, I started raising some eyebrows.

The advent of Vatican II eased the restrictions on what nuns could wear, and on many other aspects of our regimented life. However, the Good Shepherd Sisters were still set in their ways. One of the Sisters commented, "You are such a free spirit we don't know how to contain you." My inward response was, "Why should you?" But I made no comment.

I found peace in the realization that if God gives you a talent, He expects you to use it. You don't need to apologize for His gifts, only for neglecting to use them. You are honoring your Creator by making use of them. Not do so would insult His generosity. This realization gave me the courage to keep going. My drive has always been to answer the call and let God do the rest. It is with this focus that I have been able to live through my contradictions and personal doubts in order to become a runner and triathlete of quality, even if I am a nun.

Nonetheless, I am aware that there are some who may not regard my pursuit of running and triathlon as appropriate for a nun. Please know that in the initial stages I too was unsure. Never in a thousand years could I have conceived that this was a presentable choice for someone like me. Furthermore, there was no such thing as running when I entered the Convent at the age of twenty-three, only track. Triathlons were born more than forty years after I was. I could not have possibly foreseen how the future would unfold. Here the words of Christ come to mind:

"You have not chosen me, but I have chosen you" (John 15:16). Consequently I have not chosen running and triathlons—they have chosen me.

I tend to attack everything with determination and exert every fiber of my being once I am committed to a goal. Were it not for this diligence, I would never have overcome the obstacles involved in the decision to devote myself to the life of a Catholic Sister, nor to the discipline of running. But I have developed a sense of dependence on Divine assistance. It wasn't a fitness thing that got me involved in running, it was a spiritual quest. God had given me these talents, and I wanted to return the glory to Him. I feel that I must be true to my potential in order to be true to my God.

I always try to make it to daily Mass somehow. Then I feel free and open to anything that might transpire through the day. That's what makes me so light and free even when things are looking dismal. It comes from having acquired from all these years a personal relationship with God. It's not an up-in-the-sky kind of God, but someone who is very personal and intimate and with whom I can carry on a conversation throughout the day. To this day I have never missed Sunday Mass on account of a race, except on a few occasions when I have been captive on a plane. But even then I am communing with my Creator, a bond that is totally independent of time and space and can be established anywhere, at any time.

Sometimes this communing is done quite spontaneously, and takes the form of me yelling, screaming, and even laughing at God. Nonetheless, when a child kicks and screams and throws a temper tantrum, is he or she any less loved by the parent? It is thus that I am confident of my Creator's love for me despite my moods. In this way I can participate in a demanding athletic schedule while remaining faithful to my primary vocation. Knowing the Lord is ever present makes me feel as if I am being led to where I am supposed to be, at a certain time, for a certain reason. I definitely live by natural rhythms and wake up with the light rather than an alarm. With God as my constant companion, I am always in communication, even on the run. No doubt He has no problems keeping pace with me.

I do get out of kilter occasionally such as when I find myself yelling at a recorded message on the phone because I can't reach a real representative. Because I am a zodiac Leo, there are times when I roar. In most cases, it's not myself I'm defending, but someone else. I have always felt inclined to help those who are down and out. That's why I visit women in jail and work as a guardian *ad litem*. I can't right every wrong, but I can point the way toward goodness in another's life.

Over time, I have come to realize more and more how well physical activity fits into a life of prayer. In one race, I was running along chanting to myself, "Bless the Lord, praise His Holy name," when I noticed a man who seemed to be struggling. I began saying the prayer out loud. It has a good rhythm to it. I said the prayer repeatedly, and as I passed the man, I said to him, "Chant it, it will help pick up your pace!" He started repeating it, and he got a second wind. He surged ahead to the finish, but he waited for me to cross the line. Afterward he asked me if I would write down those words on the back of his race number. "I want to remember that phrase so I can keep using it," he told me.

10

Breaking the Mold

The longer I am steeped in living,
the more I marvel at its mystery.

WHEN YOU THINK about it, everything in a triathlon is very natural and childlike. You learn to balance a bike at an early age, toddlers often break into a run rather than walk, and we all floated in our mothers' wombs without fear. So what is the big deal? Some triathletes tend to get puffed up about themselves; I would like to burst their bubbles. There is really nothing exceptional about doing a triathlon, except perhaps pushing the limits of endurance, but even that can build up with time. All that we do in our sport of triathlon comes to us naturally. It is not as if we have to develop some great skill or do unusual maneuvers like gymnasts, ballet dancers, or skaters. Those are the ones who fill me with awe.

Triathlon coaches were not available when I began, and to this day I have never had one. My training is catch-as-catch-can.

I simply rely on my Creator for the signals I need and never push beyond my ability to remain upright at the finish—although there have been occasions when I have been slightly bent over in my final thrust.

I am instinctual about taking care of my body. Early on, I never thought much about food. I had grown up eating very rich foods; but in the Convent, I took whatever was served. The food was far from rich, with little seasoning, but well-planned and basic. Once I started exercising so much, I realized that I needed to take better care of myself, that proper maintenance adds to harmonic living.

Even at forty-six, before I got into running, my body had exhibited some annoying changes. I had been scrimping on my meals, gathering up leftovers when I finally got off duty. The rest of the community had already had dinner. My weakness and lethargy led to an appointment with a doctor, who suggested a six-hour glucose tolerance test. Sure enough, I was diagnosed with reactive hypoglycemia, meaning my system could not handle sugar or the equivalent well. The doctor ordered me off all sweets, including pastries and carbohydrates. The shift was too extreme for my metabolism, and my energy plummeted to an all-time low. Another physician suggested less extreme changes. Eating only proteins was obviously not agreeing with me, so he advised me to hold to a well-balanced diet, taking in some carbohydrates and fat as well.

This was a wake-up call. I became more food conscious, studying the benefits of combined fats, protein, and carbohydrates in a healthy ratio. I began to give nutrition a new respect. Now I eat simply, mostly carbohydrates and fresh vegetables and fruits. I grow my own produce in season. In colder weather, I will sometimes give in to my weaknesses—chocolate candies and chocolate chip cookies. In warmer weather I enjoy ice cream, although sometimes I substitute frozen yogurt. I eat meat with friends, but I only cook it sparingly myself, maybe twice a week. I just try to keep a well-rounded diet and throw in some vitamin supplements.

When I was in the middle of being transferred from place to place with frequently changing climates, I noticed that my knuckles were getting swollen and reddish. I figured I had been writing too much and holding my pen too tightly. I didn't think too much about it, but I had a dream in which I was told to take some Vitamin A with D, something containing fish oil. I woke up and thought, "Where did this come from?" Nonetheless, I followed the advice and went to the store for some fish oil capsules. They smelled awful, of course, but I finished the bottle and the problem went away. It might have been the beginning of arthritis. Since I have been so active, it hasn't had a chance to catch up with me again.

When I suffered from a painful blister aggravated during the 1998 Canadian Ironman, a blister that persisted for a week at the approach of the Montreal International Triathlon Union World Championship, another healing thought came to me in a dream. "Try a tea bag." Sure enough, I used a damp tea bag on the blister area overnight, and by the race day a healthy scab had formed. Nowadays I rarely go anywhere without a tea bag.

My training is my own invention and can be summarized by three principles: don't waste time training for training's sake; incorporate the workout in your daily life; make it joyful. Though reporters have quipped that I "train religiously," in reality, I've always undertrained rather than overtrained. In fact, I do what I call "functional training," using the day's demands to challenge myself physically. I take advantage of any opportunity to use my legs or wheels to literally run errands and get to my destinations. Three or four days a week, I usually swim nothing less than a mile. Some summer days I actually complete a mini triathlon getting from one place to another. When I am at home, I seldom sit down. I can be found raking leaves, planting, pulling weeds, maintaining a garden, up on the roof cleaning out gutters, or doing some other household maintenance. I'm least enthusiastic about my secretarial duties. On a daily basis, I run to Mass. If the weather isn't cooperative in the winter, I have often used snowshoes or cross-country skis to get around. Since I seem to have limited time for training, I figure that if I compete in one triathlon after another during the season, I simply get the experience of using one as training for the next.

Some people have the view that they have to get in a certain number of miles biking, running, and swimming or it's a lost day. I want to find joy in my training, so I avoid indoor training. I cannot sit on a piece of training equipment and watch those little digital numbers turn around. That's putting the machine in control, so I just have to grab my opportunities to get out in nature when I can.

I have always wanted to run with my spirit leading, not a mechanical device. Why wear yourself out when there will be a better day and you can do a better job? I don't want to get to a point where I dread training. If I do, it's time to stop. Otherwise, I am setting myself up for burnout, as I did before my transition from running to triathlons. When I was only running, there was a period when I couldn't even stand to look at a pair of running shoes. Triathlons actually saved me from the compulsiveness that can overtake runners.

I don't like to think in numbers. I feel that being focused on racking up a certain number of miles can turn me into a robot. However, there was a period during my goal-setting days when I applied visualization. In 1992, after I began participating in Ironman competitions (with their 2.4-mile swim, 112-mile bike segment, and a full 26.2-mile marathon requirement), I aimed for a time of under 13 hours in both the Canadian and Hawaiian Ironman events. I mentally concentrated on coming in around that time, but trusted my instincts since I never wear a watch. I was thrilled with my finish times of 13:16:34 for the Canadian Ironman and 13:19:01 for the Hawaiian, setting a thirteen-year record for women sixty to sixty-four. Those were my personal bests both in the same year.

Over time, I have learned to adjust what I do inside my head to the three parts of the triathlon. If composing haiku helps me with the running, concentration is the key to cycling. Out training on the bike, you have to ride defensively, always being on the lookout for the unexpected regarding traffic, pedestrians, and animals. In races, it's about self preservation. You have to be aware of what other riders are doing—or about to do—around you. But out on the open roads during long distance events, it is easy to space out. There is ample time for the mind to wander. Usually it wanders to those I'm concerned about, asking for God's intervention in their needs.

Out running or biking on my own, I still love to drink in the beauty of God's Creation, including His creatures of the wild. While biking, I've had near misses with birds, butterflies, squirrels, elk, deer, and dogs. One encounter with a pair of dogs, running wild across my path, actually brought me down and split my bike helmet.

When I am swimming in competition, I try to establish a rhythm, synchronizing my arm and leg movements, and finding my space in open water. Often I get nudged and nipped at the heels, which interrupts my rhythm. When this happens continuously it is hard to reestablish it. The swim is survival, just as is the intensity of the bike race. But the run gives me more freedom. That's when I can really settle into why I am doing this, and who I am doing it for. I let my thoughts free float. In fact, it works a lot better if I think of something else, rather than tuning in on my body exclusively. I almost always hold someone or some situation in my prayers while I am running.

In 1981 I marked twenty-five years with the Good Shepherd Sisters. My parents agreed to come to Spokane from Saint Louis to help me celebrate my silver anniversary. We met in Seattle first to tour the Olympic Peninsula. When I rented a car at the airport, the agent encouraged me to pay extra for insurance. I thought, "No, I won't need it. I am a safe driver, and I won't let anything happen to this car." So I refused the insurance.

After picking up my parents at the Seattle airport, we drove up to the Olympic Peninsula and spent a couple of nights at Quinault Lodge with its beautiful rustic ambience. The next morning we were ready to drive down to Rockaway on the Oregon coast to spend some time at the Sisters' beach house before driving on to Spokane for my anniversary ceremony.

As we started out, my mother said to my father, "Darling, are you going to let your daughter do all the driving?" My stomach hit rock bottom when I heard this. "Oh, why did she have to say that?" I thought. If I refused to let him drive, it would probably insult him, so with apprehension I turned over the wheel.

We had scarcely gone ten minutes from the lodge when a deer from the other side of the road crossed in front of us. I would have done the opposite of what my father did. He tried to steer over to the shoulder in the same direction the deer was running, but in so doing he encountered the deer. The deer was thrown to the side of the road by the impact. Mommy yelled, "Oh, dear." Daddy froze at the wheel.

I slowly opened the car door, saying, "I am going to take a look." Kneeling over the deer, her beautiful velvet eyes wide open, I said, "It's all right, my dear deer. It will be okay. You are going to go to your maker soon. Be at peace. It won't take long." I patted her on the forehead and dispensed a blessing. She seemed to relax, closed her eyes, and was gone.

I went to the car announcing that I had blessed the deer just in time, and she had died peacefully, hoping this comment would make my father feel better. We exchanged seats without a word. Daddy, being conservative, was not willing to let the meat go to waste. I stopped at the ranger station, as Daddy directed, to inform a ranger where to locate the deer. He said they didn't use road kill, but thanked us for informing them of the incident. My father was disappointed. The car radiator was damaged, so we had to stop periodically to refill it with water.

Back home Daddy tried to get his insurance to cover the matter. It took almost two years before the company decided that the incident had been "an act of God" and paid for the damage. Of course, Daddy's premiums went up as a consequence, but he was of the age where that was going to happen anyway. In hindsight, I should have taken out that insurance, but I didn't expect I'd have an alternate driver.

The year after my silver anniversary, my friend Roy Allen, who was a retired policeman and a triathlete, returned from doing the 1982 Hawaiian Ironman in Kona on the Big Island and couldn't stop talking about it. He was so enthralled that it was hard to resist his entreaties to try it. By this time I had participated in several triathlons. But an Ironman distance? That seemed a bit daunting.

But Roy insisted: "Sister, you have got to do this race!" That's how I decided to tackle a full Ironman distance in Hawaii. It was there to be done, so why not try? Of course, I had to have a certain amount of faith that I could pull it off—plus learning from my previous mistakes.

The Hawaiian Ironman seemed a fitting goal since my second triathlon was a Half Ironman. Once I set my sights on that competition, I was determined, and intended to compete just as soon as I could. But God had other plans, and it took me four years to see my dream come true.

By 1982, the Good Shepherd School for Girls in Spokane was under pressure to close its doors. The remaining six Sisters moved to an older home across town. The school itself was sold to an agency that accepted socially disadvantaged boys as well as girls. I was sent to Honolulu by the Provincial, who decided that the small home there would be a peaceful place for me to do some writing. I soon realized this must have been a part of God's plan to get me involved in the Ironman. Never would I have happened into the famed Hawaiian Ironman Triathlon without this predestined venture to Hawaii for an entirely different purpose.

Once I was in Honolulu, it suddenly dawned on me that I had no way of getting around, other than my feet. Since there was just one car available to the Sisters, it was in constant use, so I found a bike to buy from a gal who was going to upgrade to another. She was asking one hundred dollars for her Fuji but was willing to accept eighty. Biking, together with running, became my mode of transportation. Eventually I found myself working out on track with a group called the Farber Flyers, named after a local coach. I also increased my distance running around the island.

Now that I was here, I decided this was the perfect opportunity to inquire about the Ironman. I contacted the director, Valerie Silk, to ask whether I could enter it. Her first question was, "But Sister, have you ever done a race this length?"

I confidently told her I'd done a Half Ironman distance in Spokane before I left home and figured I wouldn't have a problem with a full one. I added that I'd like to do each leg for a special cause. She listened and replied, "Well, my real concern is for you, but if you really think you can, I'm willing to let you try."

It was my desire to collect pledges for three different causes, and I had already contacted the Diabetes and Heart foundations, who said they had never before been part of a combined fundraiser, and it sounded exciting. I was in the process of finding a third charity when suddenly I was recalled to Spokane. Having taken a vow of Obedience, I never asked why. The move was so abrupt I had to leave my secondhand bicycle behind. Fortunately

I found some Spokane friends who were going over for the Honolulu marathon and were willing to bring it back for me.

For that year, the Hawaii Ironman was out of the picture. But I wasn't about to give up the dream.

Before returning to Spokane, I asked permission to visit my parents in Saint Louis to celebrate their fifty-fifth wedding anniversary. While there, I wanted to keep up my training, so I borrowed a family member's bike. On a warm day in June, I set out riding through the old neighborhood I had known as a child. Going downhill on the borrowed bike, I reached for the brakes. I had never used that particular kind before and quickly found out why they were called "suicide brakes." The suddenness of the pressure flipped me over the handle bars, and I crashed against the curb. I felt something scratch the left side of my head as I hit the cement. I was not wearing a helmet, only a baseball cap. Stunned, I slowly sat up and looked around to find a big bus behind me. The quizzical look on the driver's face spoke for itself. "What should I do? Is she okay? Should I get out and help?"

At this point, a woman and her child were getting off the bus. Apparently they were on the way to the swimming pool, because they thrust a towel over my left arm and said, "Here, take this," and trotted on. "Why did they give me this?" I wondered. Seeing I had been attended to, the bus driver drove around me. I was still sprawled against the curb.

Shortly after that, a woman with a station wagon stopped and said, "You have to get out of the street. Here, let me help you get onto the lawn." When she got a closer look at me, she said, "Oh my goodness. We have to take you to the hospital. You are bleeding badly from the elbow." Now I knew the reason for the towel. I told her I had to stop by my parents' house first to drop off a key for a family member who was expecting it. She agreed to take me there. Once in the door, I went directly to the bathroom, where I noticed blood dripping onto the white tile floor. It was then I realized, yes, I was in trouble. I wrote a quick note to my parents about my whereabouts and left with the woman.

At the hospital, I waited three hours and was getting more and more hungry. It was now three o'clock, and I had had nothing to eat since breakfast. All I could envision was a strawberry milkshake. By then, my mother had come home and tracked me down at the hospital. When she heard I hadn't been seen yet, she was adamant about getting me into the hands of a doctor who had treated one of my nieces for a broken arm, which meant changing hospitals. I was taken by ambulance though I begged them not to use the siren.

I was soon in surgery, which involved placing screws in what proved to be a compound fracture of my right elbow. I was told I needed to remain in the hospital for a week.

Now that I was lying in a hospital bed, I was afraid my legs would atrophy if they didn't get a little exercise. When none of the medical staff was around, I escaped and made my way up and down eight flights in the stairwell. I sneaked back into the room, thinking I had not been missed. In the meantime, a nurse had come in to check on me and was quite alarmed when she found me missing. The doctor chided me. Because I was an apparent risk to have around, he decided to discharge me a day early, although he forbade me to attend my niece's wedding, warning, "If you get bumped in a crowd or happen to slip and fall, your elbow is a goner."

He had successfully put the fear of God into me, so I gave up on the wedding. But once at my parents' home I made my way around the neighborhood to exercise my legs. I had just three weeks before the Diet Pepsi Championship 10K on July 1 in New York, for which I had qualified. The doctor gave me permission to take the flight, and he put me in a half cast, cautioning me to avoid crowds. I didn't tell him I was actually about to be joining a crowd—a crowd on the move.

When I showed up with my encased arm, the Diet Pepsi committee said, "You are welcome to attend the banquet and just be a spectator if you like." I answered, "No thank you, I would really like to run. What if I just put a sign on my back saying, '*Beware, injured runner, no passing on right.*'" Laughing, they agreed and gave me my race packet.

Race morning was cool and drizzly, so I was extra cautious, but I also needed to move at a rate that would keep me from getting too chilled. Only two people passed me on the right, and I ended up doing the 10K in sufficient time to take fourth place in my age group among woman from all over the country.

11

Triathlon Trials and Triumphs

You're never too old to learn, so you're never too old to "tri."

THE 1983 HAWAIIAN Ironman was now three months away. But when I finally returned to our Convent in Spokane, I was informed by the Provincial that I was not to return to Hawaii—no explanation given. I wouldn't be able to accept the invitation to do the Hawaiian Ironman after all. I was baffled and disappointed, but tried to accept the decision.

I reset my goal and decided to attempt the Hawaiian Ironman again in 1984. With my bike still in Hawaii, I needed to resume training. Again the benefactor of the Good Shepherd Sisters who had gotten me my first pair of running shoes came to the rescue by purchasing a green Centurion bike from a police auction for my first triathlon. Neither he nor I knew anything about sizing. It was a man's bike with the top bar at least an inch higher than it should have been. It took all the courage I had to get on it after my accident. But once astride, I pedaled around a fifteen-mile hilly course around Newman Lake.

On September 8, with the 1984 Hawaiian Ironman just a month away, I decided to bike out to Liberty Lake near the Idaho border to squeeze in an open-water swim. This was about a forty-mile round trip. On my return from the lake, the traffic had picked up because of rush hour, and I got tired of dismounting every block, so decided to take another route. As I was crossing a wide intersection, a car came up from behind the cars already stopped. The signal changed when I was only halfway across, but this car kept moving, crossing directly in front of me. I was on a friend's bike and did not want it damaged. "Oh, God, what should I do now?"

There was nothing to do but swerve to my left to avoid hitting the car broadside, barely missing it. The turn was too abrupt, and I landed on my left hip, and I felt something slide as I did so. Instinctively, I said, "There goes the Ironman for the second time. God, what have you got against me doing the Ironman, anyway?" I didn't know what damage was done, but I knew that the race, just a month away, was out of the question.

I was in acute pain when the ambulance attendants moved me onto a stretcher. The X-rays revealed a broken hip at the femur and a fracture down the shank. The doctor said he had to operate on someone else immediately and that if he was not finished by eight o'clock that evening, we would have to delay my surgery until Saturday. This was Friday, and they were short-staffed on the weekend. He seemed tense and weary, and I thought, "Lord, maybe he shouldn't do it tonight after all. I wanted him to be fresh and on top of things." As I lay there waiting to learn what was in store, an orderly came into the room. Without a word he attached some contraption to the foot of my bed and then to my leg. All of a sudden he gave it a yank, and I let out a yelp that would have been enough to send my roommate flying out of her bed if she had been able. Without a word, he left the room.

The next morning, around eleven o'clock, the doctor came and announced that he had had a chance to review the X-rays. "It appears that the fracture is on the tip of the femur, and there is no guarantee the screw will hold. You may never be able to walk again." I looked at him in dismay. All I could muster was, "What are the options?" He simply shrugged his shoulders as if to say, "There are none."

My response was, "Well, let's just go for it and see what happens." He replied, "If that is your desire, but I am not sure when the operating room will be available. It may be a long wait." I could tell he was apprehensive, so I said, "Doc, go out and have a good run for me." He responded seriously, "Not on your life." He said he had to wait there until the operating room was free. Another three hours went by. A friend and her daughter came a marathon's distance to visit and pray over me. I suggested we also pray for the doctor.

Five minutes after my friends left, the nurse came in, threw a sheet over me, and hauled me down to the catacomb level. The doctor was waiting there in surgical attire. As the nurse was pushing me past him on the way to surgery, I waved and said, "Doc, you've just been prayed for that you'll have a steady hand and a clear mind." His response was, "Humppph!"

I awoke from a two-and-a-half-hour surgery to find him standing at the foot of my bed. The tenseness was gone. "The operation was a success," he said. He explained that the break was not as close to the end of the femur as he had originally thought. He'd been able to attach a Swedish screw to the plate running down my shank, and the fracture there was not as long as he had originally feared either. The plate, he said, was held in by five pins. "Your bone was so strong that it even bent the middle pin." When I asked how all this would impede my progress as far as running went, he simply shrugged.

Released from the hospital on crutches and with a prescription to prevent swelling, I was told to keep my foot elevated above my head. There was very little I could do in this position. The next day was Sunday, but my leg had gotten so swollen that I consulted the doctor on call. He suggested I come to emergency immediately. "We may have to test you for phlebitis," he said. Such was the case, and I was sent home with compression stockings and another prescription.

Providentially, while I was laid up, one of our Sisters suggested I spend my time reading *Sudden Spring* by Lillana Kopp, a former Holy Name Sister. This kept me occupied. The book described a new type of Sisterhood designed according to the promulgations of Vatican II set forth by Pope John Paul XXIII. Instead of the hierarchical structure of our traditional Orders, it suggested that decisions be made by consensus, with all members having a say. It also encouraged Sisters to go out into the world and find their own ministry.

Founded in 1970, just fourteen years before my accident, this group called the Sisters for Christian Community seemed a Godsend. The concept of making decisions by consensus appealed to me, and I was eager to be involved in the world at large. I missed working with troubled girls, and without such an apostolate, the Sisters tended to focus on themselves rather than on the work for which the Order was originally founded, caring for girls gone astray. Under these circumstances, being a nun felt like belonging to a sorority. I preferred to depend on the Holy Spirit to lead me. This new approach I read about gave me fresh hope and felt right for me. I began to give the ideas suggested in the book serious thought, praying for discernment. The whole tenor of Religious Life was evolving along with societal changes.

And, yes, God certainly knows how to catch our attention. Had it not been for this enforced nonactivity, I would never have been still long enough to have devoured *Sudden Spring*. As it turned out, the effects of this book would redirect the rest of my life.

A transfer from a traditional Order to a less restrictive one is not an easy matter. It took a few years before Papal permission was granted, and I became a fully fledged member of the Sisters for Christian Community. Once this was accomplished, I felt more like an adult taking responsibility for myself and involved in the world around me. Since the other Good Shepherd Sisters were soon to leave Spokane, I decided to remain and live alone, seeking various ways to minister to others. The Sisters in my new Order supported me. They, too, were moving with the times. At first it seemed strange to live alone without any set regulations, but I soon got used to my own company and have lived in the same spot in a mobile park situated on the Spokane River since 1991.

My involvement in running and triathlons had by then developed into a sense of community that helped me during this transition period. I felt at home meeting athletes on their own turf and sweating it out with them. But I was still coping with the emotional upheaval of having left what had been my spiritual home for nearly thirty years, when along came another loss.

In 1984, my father, at age eighty-three, had just had his first cataract surgery. He called me to announce that he had just "seen" Ronald Reagan sworn in for his second presidency, and he was jubilant. In a matter of a few weeks, he underwent his second cataract surgery, which did not go well. When they removed the patch, his eye was bloodshot. He noticed the exchange of looks between my mother and the doctor. This signaled to him, "Not so good."

Three days later, I got a call from one of my brothers saying that Daddy had died. I was devastated. With heavy heart, I made arrangements to go home for his funeral. Now I had no one left for me to make proud. My mother had never really approved of my athletic pursuits. Not only was she concerned that this was not setting forth the right image for a nun, but she considered it too risky for her darling daughter.

I mourned the loss of my father, knowing I would miss his subtle encouragement. That feeling together with the loss of my original Order, the Sisters of the Good Shepherd, stripped me of any sense of belonging. I had to grope in this darkness for quite a while. Finally I came to grips with the fact that I was totally and utterly dependent on the Lord for my grounding. I belonged completely to Him.

In 1985 I decided to attempt the Hawaiian Ironman once more. The race was scheduled for October, and in August I went to Australia to visit a friend whom I had met while she was taking a course at Gonzaga University in Spokane. She too had left her former Order and was venturing out for herself back in her homeland. While in Australia, I heard about a marathon there and decided to enter it as training for the Ironman.

But nearly four years after my hip surgery, I was still limping. I had not realized that when I got off of crutches, I wouldn't be able to get out and walk normally. This had been a jolt to my system. Nonetheless, I limped my way through the marathon and was elated just to be able to do that much. I was almost resigned to the fact that I would limp for the rest of my life, but at least I was moving. After my broken hip, the doctors had never really given me the go-ahead to engage in these activities again. So I just went out and did it.

With my eyes set on the Ironman, I was also doing some training on the bike while in Australia. On one of these rides in late afternoon, with the setting sun in my eyes, I suddenly felt myself being rammed from the rear by an automobile. It catapulted me into the air. As I was coming down, I prayed, "O God, this one looks like a five-point landing so no broken bones, please." However, when I tried to sit up, there seemed to be a little crunching in my midsection. The woman who hit me was distraught and rushed me to the hospital. Australia is a great place to be admitted to a hospital, as it turned out. The nurses did not even ask my name, but simply attended to me. They found I had broken ribs, a contusion in my right leg, and a chipped heel.

I had scarcely a month left in Australia before leaving for Hawaii, so I kept exercising the best I could with these impediments. Because of my unstable ribs, I decided to train in a pool rather than the ocean. But I couldn't do any running because of the injured leg. As soon as I got to Hawaii, a few days before the Ironman, I went to the doctor to get a cortisone shot. It was tricky for him to find just the right spot for the injection since my leg was still swollen, and he jabbed me in three places, hoping to hit the mark.

The day before the big race, all the competitors gathered on the lawn of the host hotel for an orientation meeting. Besides the usual briefing, the race director, Kay Rhead, informed us that a hurricane was scheduled to hit the Big Island the next day. She was so deadpan in her announcement, we were not sure if she was serious. It turned out there really was a hurricane warning, but it veered off into the ocean, leaving swells two to four feet high and a strong current for the swim portion of the race.

Once the race was underway, I forgot about my ribs. But after a while in the water, I could not see any other swimmers around me. The man escorting me on a surfboard was yelling at me, but I could not make out what he was saying. I assumed he was trying to tell me to step up the pace. As I got close to the pier, I felt I was swimming in place. The scenery below me never changed. When I finally emerged from the water, I was told I was four minutes beyond the cutoff time of two hours and fifteen minutes and would not be allowed to complete the Ironman. Had the cutoff time been what it is today, two hours and twenty minutes, I would have been allowed to go on.

My hands felt like prunes, and my body was shaking. Before I could even recover from my discouragement, someone thrust a microphone in my face. All I could say was that I was sorry I could not use the bike that had been donated to me for the purpose of doing the Ironman. I returned to the hotel to shower and wash the salt water from my hair, thinking all the while of the lyrics from South Pacific: "I'm gonna wash that man right outta my hair . . ." Then I went back to retrieve my bike from the transition area. I got on it figuring enough time had elapsed so they would not mistake me as one of the competitors. I would just ride out to encourage the others who were still racing as they were coming back.

About twelve miles out, I realized I hadn't taken any food or water. "Lord," I prayed, "I need some provisions. I'm getting hungry and I have a way to go." At this point, a man from the aid station on the opposite side of the road happened to turn around and spot me. Without a word from me he ran over and handed me a banana. "Surely an angel in disguise," I thought.

I rode on, figuring I would get a good idea of what the bike course was like as well as cheering people on. When I was fourteen miles short of the bike turnaround in Hawi, I noticed a staff van perched on the side of the hill. How in the world did they get there? I saw them looking down at me so called up, "Do you think the aid station is still open at the turnaround?" They yelled back, "We doubt it."

I continued up the hill for another three miles until I noticed a lone Japanese rider descending. I figured he was probably the last participant. If that was the case, there was no reason for me to go any further so I turned around. By now, the staff car had maneuvered off the side of the mountain and was on the road in front of me. Since my number was still on the bike, they probably had had a chance to check me out, realizing I was no longer in the race, and asked, "Would you like a ride back? Or something to eat or drink?"

"Yes," I replied.

"Which one?" they asked.

"All three!"

By now I had traveled about fifty miles on one banana, so

riding in the van with the comfort of some food and drink to alleviate my weary, overheated body was a relief. Listening to the play-by-play account on the radio also made me feel as if I was still part of the race.

As the staffers were chatting, they said, "Do you know there is a Priest out there?" I said, "Do you mean the Episcopalian minister?" They pointed him out as we passed, and I took note of his race number. He was the same Priest who had not made the bike cutoff the year before. Now I saw he was trailing the Japanese rider I had seen coming down from Hawi.

A few miles ahead, I asked the driver to let me out. I wanted to get on my bike and ride the rest of the way in. I didn't tell them I intended to encourage the Priest. As I got on my bike, I said, "Oh, there he goes, I'll never catch him." They said, "Oh, yes you will. You will catch him on the hill."

That was exactly where I came up beside him. As he was struggling, I said, "Hello, Padre. Would you like to hear my confession?" He looked at me very quizzically, so I thought I'd better introduce myself properly. In acknowledgment he pointed to a little sign on his bike stem that said, "Go for God."

Shortly after that, a truck with someone hanging out of the tailgate yelled angrily at us. I was wondering what that was about. Then the Padre made a sudden move to go around me. We had been riding side by side. Suddenly it dawned on me that I could possibly disqualify him, by putting him in the position of drafting me. That I did not want to do, so I pulled up ahead of him, remaining in sight so I could be his carrot on the string.

When I found myself closing in on the Japanese guy, I yelled, "You better step it up. There is a Padre behind you ready to pass."

Then I dropped back a little and shouted to the Padre, "You've got to pass that Japanese guy up front!"

As we neared the airport and the turnaround for the runners on the course, the aid stations on both sides of the road had people out in the middle of the course, passing out nourishment. I thought, "Egads, we could be knocked off our bikes as their backs were toward us. I had better tunnel my way through this area and yell, 'Bikers coming! Bikers coming!' until we gain safe passage through this sea of humanity." Thus it was that we passed through without incident.

About a mile and a half from the bike finish, we faced a very steep hill. Concerned about the Padre's stamina, I decided to barrel up it, inspiring him to do the same. At the crest, I dismounted to wait for him, anxious because time was really running out. Finally I saw the top of his head and knew he had gotten off his bike to foot it up the hill. When he finally got to the top, I yelled, "Come on, Padre! There's no time to lose!" and pedaled hard. He made it to the bike finish with only a few minutes to spare.

It was now dark, and I realized I had no headlights on my bike and would be in jeopardy heading back into town with crowds crisscrossing back and forth. I did not want to be toppled off my bike once again. I waited until the Padre started out on the run, and yelled, "Padre, you're on your own now. Go for God!"

The next morning I checked the results to find that he had been the last official finisher, two minutes shy of the seventeen-hour cutoff. My mission had been accomplished. I did not finish the race, but I had helped another to do it. In a Christmas letter that year, he thanked me for being his angel escort.

12

Iron Spirit

People always ask me how I'm able to compete in the
Ironman competitions at my age and do so well.
I have a very simple answer: I don't know.

THE NEXT YEAR, 1986, I attempted the Hawaiian Ironman once
again, traveling first to Australia, to enjoy another visit with my
friend and to compete in the World Cup Triathlon in Perth. I
got to Hawaii this time in fine shape, with no physical problems,
geared to give it my all.

The swim and bike ride went well, and I was running on the
Queen Kam Highway before dark set in. The sun dips below
the horizon abruptly at six o'clock. I decided to play a game
with myself, breaking stride, to see if I could walk as fast as the
woman running in front of me and catch up with her. When I
came alongside her, she glanced at me with a dazed expression.
I touched her forehead and found she was feverish. Since she
didn't speak English, I made motions to indicate that she should
drink some water, and I slowed to walk with her.

A runner going the opposite direction, coming back from the turnaround toward the finish, called over to me asking whether anything was the matter. I yelled that we needed water. Not long after that, he doubled back with a bottle of water. By then, I had pulled an aspirin out of my pocket and motioned for the woman to take it with the water. She complied, but I wondered if we could get to an aid station soon enough as she obviously needed attention. Just then, an ambulance came up alongside us and I motioned for her to get in. Fortunately she did, and I was able to continue. Now that I was free to carry on with my race, I realized I could still finish in a good time if I picked it up. I finished with a time of 14:31:58—an age-group record for women fifty-five to fifty-nine.

Next year when I flew to Hawaii for the 1987 Ironman, a sense of forboding gripped me. The Big Island, more than any other, reveals Mother Nature's power in full. The heat from scorched lava beds and the testy trade winds can be merciless. It usually just inspires me to respect the Creator, but this year I had a strange premonition about the race.

A week before the event I was out training on my bike. As I was returning from an arduous ride, my vision blurred by sweat and fatigue, I recognized the figure running along the road as Pat Griskus. He, in turn, called out my name, and I reached out my hand to salute him as we passed. Pat was an ex-Marine who had lost his left leg during a motorcycle accident while he was on duty in Germany. He was in tip-top physical shape, competing with an artificial limb. This was to be his third Ironman. He was well known by the triathlete community for his courage and his determination not to let his infirmity keep him from being recognized as an elite athlete.

Because he wanted this year's event to be his best ever, Pat had come over to train a month early. Robin, his wife, was to join him several days before the race with their baby daughter. His smile was always engaging, even in the midst of competition, when you knew he was hurting. Even so an indomitable spirit was etched on his face.

The next day when I was out on my bike, I was overtaken midway on a hill by an Australian woman and her companion who told me that my rear wheel was wobbling. They offered to stop and take a look, but I yelled back and suggested we complete our climb first. We stopped at the top of the hill at a scenic point to have a look. A young Asian man was there too, poised on a rock wall with his bike propped against it gazing out at the ocean. He seemed engulfed in thought.

After looking over my wheel, the Australians told me that there was nothing they could do. The wheel was either bent or the spokes needed truing, and they didn't have the proper tools. By now, our presence apparently had interrupted the young man's solitude and he turned to see what was going on. He didn't speak English but assessed the situation. Wordlessly he got out a spoke wrench from his pack and spent the next twenty minutes bent over in the hot sun, trying to make the needed adjustments as ardently as if it were his own bike. Finally, he made gestures indicating that I needed to go to the bike shop for further work.

Dave's Bike Shop was en route, so I stopped there and had Dave give my wheel a once-over. His probing revealed a rim that had been bent from mishandling during my journey. "So I need a new wheel, Dave?" He asked those who had dropped in if they happened to have an extra wheel to lend me. But a fellow triathlete by the name of Bob Mason, who knew me, happened to be in the shop too, and pulled Dave aside. Before I could even negotiate with Dave, Bob had paid for a new wheel.

I realized I'd been the recipient of at least four acts of kindness, all within an hour's time—the Australian couple's concern, the young cyclist's mechanical help, Dave's expertise, and now, Bob's generosity. These acts certainly served to renew my faith in the innate goodness of our human nature. I felt blessed by these contacts.

The mood changed quickly however when another cyclist bounded through the door and shocked us with the announcement that he had just passed a spot where a cyclist had been hit. Upon further questioning, it sounded as if the accident had been fatal, because a white sheet had been thrown over the body. The man who'd come upon the scene could not say who the victim was, but said he had noticed an artificial limb lying out in the road several yards beyond the body.

Gasping, I immediately thought of Pat Griskus, whom I had just seen the day before. Dave called the hospital, and though they would not release the name or condition, Dave said, "I can tell by the way they talked that it was probably fatal." We sat there motionless. Finally, with heavy hearts, Bob and I left the shop. Bob too had just had contact with Pat the day before, during a practice swim.

When the sad news was confirmed, I couldn't let the matter rest. I felt in my heart that something had to be done to honor Pat and lift the spirits of the triathletes. I knew how many people would be distressed by this tragedy. After consulting a few people about my idea, I called the race director, Kay Rhead, to get permission to carry a sign in the Ironman parade in memory of Pat. She hesitated at first, saying she really guarded against doing anything bizarre. I didn't let this remark deter me and went on to explain what I had in mind, telling her that I already had checked it out with some other triathletes to get a sense of how they felt about it. All seemed to be in agreement. Finally she said, "Well, let me put it this way. I won't stand in the way of anything the triathletes want to do."

In the parade, a couple who had befriended me one day at the pier walked on either side of me. Together we had fashioned a wooden placard bearing the message around the sides of a triangle (symbol of both triathlon and the Holy Trinity): *Pat Griskus is still with us.* At the base it said, *His spirit lives.* On the back was a simple cross with Pat's race number at the foot. We expected to line up in front of the U.S. triathletes, but when I got there, Kay signaled for me to go to the front of the entire contingent. Thus Pat's tribute led the procession.

The night before the race another young triathlete from Arizona joined me and the couple to drive out to the site where the accident happened in order to plant the memorial placard. Having no tools we took turns picking up rocks, using them to hammer the wooden stakes into the hard lava until we finally got the sign inserted. We added three more signs spaced apart, each one bearing the message from Saint Paul (from 2 Timothy 4:7) *I have fought the good fight, I have finished the race, I have kept the faith.*

A jar was placed down by the pier where triathletes trained for the swim so they could donate toward a scholarship fund for Pat's eight-month-old daughter. His wife, who had planned to come over to see Pat race, courageously decided to carry through with her plan following his death. Strips of black ribbon had been given out for the athletes to wear in honor of Pat. On race day, I tied mine to the strap on my right shoulder.

During the actual race, as I was coming back on the bike ride with eighteen miles yet to go, I glanced toward the spot where we had placed the placard. At this very point where I caught sight of it, my black ribbon, which had been trailing behind me, all of a sudden flew up over my shoulder and across my heart. I took this as a sign that Pat approved of our intentions to honor him. This 1987 Ironman, though tearful, was also triumphant.

I had nearly reached the turnaround on the marathon portion when I noticed a man bent over, heaving up his guts. I stopped to see if I could help. He straightened up and said, "I gotta finish."

"Finish you will," I told him, "if you just walk a while, instead of run. The aid station isn't far away. I'll run ahead and get you some water." When I brought it back, he had straightened up and was walking so I gave him the water and continued running.

With about eight miles left to go, my right foot began feeling very funny. I was trying out a pair of shoes that I thought might hasten my transition because they were easier to get on and out of, but it turned out they lacked adequate foot support for a marathon distance. Eventually I had to walk and skip, favoring my right foot. As I was limping along, Roy Allen, the man from my hometown of Spokane who had introduced me to the Hawaiian Ironman, came running up behind me and said, "C'mon, Sister, we've got to start running!" He apparently was wearing a watch and knew that to requalify for the next year's race, those in our age group had to finish within fifteen hours.

I said, "Roy, can't you see I can't run? Something's wrong with my foot." He responded, "Yeah, I've got blisters and it's hard for me to run, too, but let's go." We toed the finish line together in 14:58:14. Whew! That was a close call!

A week after I got home, I decided I better go to the doctor, only to find out that I had been running with a fractured metatarsal bone. It would take time to heal, but I had made it through this year's Ironman. Winter was now setting in on Spokane so the timing was right to give my foot a chance to heal.

The 1988 Hawaiian Ironman was no less painful. The night before the race I had retired early, but I was awakened at ten o'clock by the phone ringing. I hoped the owners of the condo, who slept below my loft, would answer. However, on the third ring I decided it was my responsibility. So I wound myself down the spiral staircase from the loft in the dark and dashed across the room for the phone in my bare feet, encountering a wooden chest along the way. I grabbed the phone and managed a painful "hello" but, adding insult to injury, the person on the other end hung up at that precise moment. I hobbled to the refrigerator for some ice, and spent a wakeful night icing my toes.

By morning, my two toes were swollen and felt no better. As I lay by the poolside of the King Kamehameha Hotel waiting for the race to start, I wondered if I should back out. When I mentioned my misgivings to the person sitting next to me, he advised, "Well, why not start the swim? You can always turn back if you can't make it." That sounded reasonable enough, so into the ocean I went at the signal of the conch shell.

Once in the water, I found it painful to kick, but I got so absorbed in trying to find my space in the water that I concentrated solely on that instead of on my foot. Somehow I got through the swim and ventured onto the bike. But at mile 13, the pain was such that when I spotted a Red Cross wagon at a scenic turnout, I decided to get a professional opinion. They took a look at my foot and told me I probably had two broken toes, and there was nothing they could do except give me aspirin for the pain. They cautioned that it would take about twenty minutes before I felt any relief, and said if it was still too painful they would pick me up to bring me in.

I took at least ten aspirin throughout that long day—overdose, you might say. Halfway through the run, the foot pain was agonizing. Spotting friends on the sidelines, I asked them to tell the announcer to please ask the crowd to pray for Sister Madonna, that she can finish with two broken toes. Somehow I was able to toe the finish, but it was the slowest Ironman I had ever done to that point—16:18:20. A long, long day!

By now I was beginning to wonder if I would ever do an Ironman without an incident.

13

On a Wing and a Prayer

You never know who your angels will be.

BY THE LATE 1980s, I had traveled extensively—to Hawaii, Australia, Canada, as well as all over the United States, from California's wine country to Florida's Gulf coast. Within a period of twelve years, these triathlons that had been relatively quiet events boomed into crowded extravaganzas. The number of people involved in marathons and triathlons mushroomed. Before long, I settled on certain annual races either because they were particularly well organized or because I liked the enthusiasm of the participants. Also a number of race directors were willing to waive my entry fees, including Valerie Silk, previous owner of the Hawaiian Ironman. At least seven directors have done this for me over the years, so I try to honor their generosity by returning to their races whenever possible. Over time, I've become something of a weather mascot during these events, which can be testy due to iffy conditions so the race directors are always glad to see me, knowing I will help intercede on their behalf.

A typical early season circuit would include the Mount Rainier Duathlon in western Washington in mid-April, then the Saint Anthony's Triathlon in Saint Petersburg, Florida, at the end of April. A week later I would move on to do Beat the Beast, a Half Ironman triathlon in Saint Croix, Virgin Islands; and then double back for the Gulf Coast Half Ironman in Panama City, Florida, the following week. By then it was time for Memphis in May, which was followed by the Saint Louis Senior Olympics and, finally, the duathlon in Sylvania, Ohio.

Some of the male competitors have their wives to act as their Sherpas. I usually plan my own travels. Frequently there are gaps in getting from point A to point B, but I trust that once I get my foot out of the door, God will provide. Relying on Him has always worked. I've always found a place to stay—whether it is a tent, on someone's sofa, or bedding down in my own car. Sometimes I have felt like Abraham wandering in the desert, but my trust has never been betrayed. God is a great "travel agent," and I have met wonderful people along the way.

Once I got into triathlons, I soon learned that hauling my bike was an athletic feat all its own. I had to break it down and pack it in a box for travel, then reassemble it when I got to the race. It required me to be a grease monkey and a mechanic. I had to learn to handle bike tools and come up with innovative solutions when things went wrong. On top of that, there was always the challenge of getting the bike box to the check-in counter while dragging my other luggage as well. Becoming a beast of burden has actually been harder than the events since I have no caddy or Sherpa.

On one flight, I had hauled my bike box into the airport and checked in, only to be told that the bike box wouldn't fit on the luggage conveyer belt. Furthermore, the agent was telling me there was no way I was going to make the plane with my messed-up ticket that reflected a number of changes. Finally, he said, "Well we might get your body on the plane, but I don't know about your luggage." Looking at my bike box, he asked, "What's in that?" I knew if I told him it was a bike, it would further detain me, so I prayed, "God, give me the right words to say, because I don't want to lie." Then I blurted, "Oh, just equipment." What kind of equipment, he wanted to know. "Oh, wheels, tools, shoes." He said, "Well, okay," and waved me on.

When I reached Spokane, my bags, including my bike box, were already waiting for me. My "travel agent" had come through again. Of course, this was all before 9/11. Strangely enough, in my travels since with all the scrap metal I carry in my body due to repair from accidents, only once have I ever gotten the wand at an airport. I guess the doctors used the right alloy to repair my parts.

Angels have appeared from everywhere. Once when an airport van that was supposed to take me to the airport failed to show up at the hotel lobby, I ran to the concierge and told him my dilemma. "I have a plane that is leaving soon and some heavy luggage to board." Just then a man came in to use the phone. I noticed he had a nice-sized vehicle, so I approached him. "Sure, I'll drop you off at the airport," he agreed. So he did.

When my friend Barbara Larrain and I were driving from Portland to the Vineman event in northern California, we stopped at an out-of-the-way gas station in the boondocks of California's agricultural area. Before continuing our journey I had gotten some popcorn, but needed to use the rest room. Since it was rather dingy looking, I decided to leave the popcorn on the curb, but took my wallet in with me. As I was leaving I was distracted by this bare-chested, bare-footed, long-haired, heavily bearded man, waiting his turn to go in and concentrated on retrieving my popcorn from the curb before dashing to the car.

Later, in Santa Rosa, when we were preparing to pick up our packets for the race which was to begin early the next day, I needed my USA Triathlon license to present, which was in my wallet. My wallet! My wallet! Where was it? I could not find it anywhere. The last time I remembered using the wallet was two hundred miles away at the remote gas station. My friend and I didn't even know the name of the station, but found out it was the only one in that small town. The woman who answered my phone call told me, "Yes, someone turned in a wallet the day before." I knew who it must have been. We picked up the wallet on our return trip. Everything was intact. You can never judge angels by their covers. Some come barefoot and bare-chested—like John the Baptist.

On another occasion, when my car ran out of gas on the Olympic Peninsula, I stood waving my arms, but car after car passed me by. Finally one car came to a stop. It was a clunker of a station wagon with a man's foot hanging out the back window along with some fishing poles. When one of the men stuck his head out of the window saying, "Now ma'am, we'd like to help you. What can we do?" I thought, "Oh, God, these guys have been drinking."

They promised to go fetch some gas and be right back, but I had my doubts. I sat there patiently praying and finally heard chug, chug, chug. Here they came! They got my car started by pouring some of the gas on the carburetor first. When I asked what I could give them for their trouble, the driver said, "Not a dime, Ma'am," offering me a can of beer, which he opened before my very eyes. I thought to myself, "So, angels also come in the guise of drunken fishermen. Do you suppose that is why St. Peter couldn't make his catch of the day?"

On another occasion when a friend who was visiting me from Walla Walla and I were driving to evening Mass, all of a sudden my car stopped dead about a mile and a half from church. I was to be a lector and do the scripture reading, so it was necessary for me to get there on time. We got out, and while we were pondering our dilemma, wondering if we could possibly foot it in time, a man suddenly appeared from nowhere asking, "Are you having trouble with your car?"

"Ah, yes," I replied "Are you a mechanic?" As he lifted the hood, he responded, "No, I'm a carpenter." He proceeded to pull up the dry oil stick. "Here's your problem." He dropped the hood and was gone instantly. My friend and I stared at each other with the same thought in mind.

We left the car and started to walk to church on opposite sides of the street, thumbing it to see who would be picked up first. We got to church in just the nick of time and found someone there who was willing to drive us back to my house afterwards, where my friend had left her car. We bought a can of oil and eventually retrieved my car. This seems to be how angels work. They are there, and then they aren't. No logical explanation. Some are friends and others complete unknowns, but always there in times of need.

Sometimes it's just mind over matter. In the 1986 New Zealand Ironman, before the introduction of wet suits into triathlon events, I lost feeling in the whole right side of my body during the 2.4-mile swim. I knew I still had twenty minutes to go in the water before I reached shore, so I began praying. "Lord, I know that our movements are controlled by our minds, so please let me swim with my brain since I cannot feel my body any longer." Next thing I knew, I had forgotten my frozen, flailing arms and legs, and I swam to shore with my brain, albeit I spent thirteen minutes in transition thawing out. Even the coffee jumped out of my cup, I was shivering so badly.

Travel has led me to some strange places. When a plane arrived late at the airport in Greensboro, North Carolina, because of thunderstorms, my connecting flight was cancelled and there wasn't another flight out until the following morning. It seemed hardly worth it to leave the airport and go searching for a place to stay as it was already late at night. I watched most travelers go on their way, and then saw a gate that seemed to be under construction. "Well," I thought, "no one will be working tonight anyway, so I'll just lie down on this wooden structure and sleep awhile on these plastic bubbles."

Every time I shifted in my sleep a plastic bubble would pop, so it was a lively night for me. Still, I managed to catch a few winks before a man came to vacuum. By then I had to go to the bathroom, but I waited until he was in the men's room, then snuck into the women's. Perhaps the toilet flush raised his suspicions, and he alerted security.

The next thing I knew, there were flashlights shining all around me and a uniformed woman was asking me how I got there. I told her my plane had been canceled so I was just waiting to catch the first one out in the morning. It was now about three o'clock in the morning. She sent me back to the main part of the terminal. Luckily I found some benches I could occupy. I decided to go to the baggage area just to see if my bike was there. Sure enough! It was standing there all alone. It was then I realized I would probably have to recheck it for my flight in the morning. Had it not been for this interruption of my sleep, I might not have discovered it.

Then I settled myself on a bench. When anyone came up to check me out, I pretended to be asleep. Eventually someone nudged me and said, "Lady, Lady. I need some identification." Supposing I looked quite haggard, I pulled out my driver's license and murmured, "I'm not sure I still look like this photo anymore after being stuck here all night." The officials asked where I had spent the night. When I motioned to the closed area, they threw up their hands in dismay. Even though I arrived home quite exhausted, at least I avoided being hauled off to jail.

The more competitions I have done, the more amazing people I have met. These events always become "a community of spirits." We are all suffering together, undergoing the same tensions, trials, and triumphs. There's an amazing give and take, which keeps me in touch with the beauty and beast of our human condition. The drama of the triathlons reveals the rawness of our nature, alternating between pain and exhilaration.

When I lay on the road after being swept off my bike during the 2000 Hawaiian Ironman, I could never forget how those two other participants, Nancy Taubner and Bill Hoon, gave up their own chance of finishing this cherished event to stay by my side until the ambulance arrived. A year later, I was able to repay this kindness by getting the race director to accept them both into the 2001 Hawaiian Ironman without having to re-qualify. Thus, the three of us were able to compete together again that following year.

In the thirty or so years that I have been running marathons and doing triathlons and competing in Ironman events, I have done a lot of damage to my body. Beyond the wreckage of the 2000 Hawaiian Ironman, I had a shoulder injury in 2006 while skiing on Mount Spokane, and have broken both elbows, suffered a broken hip, fingers, toes, a fractured jaw and scapular, plus numerous other glitches and stitches. But in every instance, I also experienced some extraordinary act of kindness.

As the saying goes, "What goes around comes around." I take this to mean that we are to be open transmitters of God's grace, allowing the current of His love to run through us to others no matter the circumstances. Because God lives in us and through us, we are capable of reaching out to others. Thus it is His grace channeled through us that inspires others we meet.

In one Canadian Ironman, when I could no longer push my body to run—I don't know if it was dehydration or my acid reflux acting up under stress—I found myself quite alone in the dark after the sun had set. I was just heading into the last stretch and still had five or six miles to go, when a staff car behind me helped to light my way and the occupants tried to carry on a conversation. That was the last thing I wanted. But then a gal hopped out of the car and said just the right thing: "I know it feels pretty lonely out here. Do you mind if I walk with you?"

I told her I was a little disappointed because this had been my chance to set a third age group record for women, and she said, "Sister, when you finish, you'll be the oldest female finisher. You *are* setting a record." And she didn't say *if*, she said *when*. I finished and achieved that goal.

You never know who you'll meet or what they'll say or do to encourage you along the way. In my lifetime, there have been periods of darkness when I felt alone, when my self-confidence was rocked to the core and I faced self-doubt on many levels. Fortunately, during my darkest periods someone has often emerged who believed in me. Everyone needs someone to believe in them.

In 1989 I competed at the inaugural International Triathlon Union World Championship in Avignon, France. The race was an Olympic distance (1.5K swim, 40K bike, and 10K run), and the swim took place in the Rhône River under historic bridges with stone buttresses. To avoid butting into them, I swam closer to shore, along a section of river where houseboats were anchored. I went on to do well in the bike segment and the run, and took first place in my age group. There were just a few others. It seemed that all of us were from the USA in this 50–59 age group.

Three weeks later, I prepared to do the Canadian Ironman in Penticton and had been invited to attend a tea with the premier of British Columbia, who had come from Vancouver to view the event. While walking to the tea house, I felt a strange gurgling in my stomach and realized I was very bloated.

After the race, a friend from Spokane who had come to watch told me she was concerned because my complexion had turned gray. I felt very feverish afterwards. When I returned to Spokane, I was still feeling under the weather, but I ignored the rumblings in my stomach and began planning to leave for Hilton

Head, South Carolina, where the USA Triathlon Championship was to be held in September. However, the race was postponed for a month because Hurricane Gloria had left devastation in its wake. I used the extra time to go see my doctor, who ordered some tests.

It wasn't until I returned from that race, however, that I learned the medical verdict. My doctor told me I had contracted giardia, a parasite that sabotages the intestinal tract. It was now November and I told him I had just come back from doing a championship triathlon in Hilton Head; before that I had completed the Canadian Ironman at the end of August; and before that the world championship in Avignon, France, on August 6, where I probably had picked up the disease while swimming in the Rhône. This meant I had already been carrying those little critters for three months.

The doctor said, "You have being doing *what*? And this swim you mention was back in early August and it is now mid-November? Do you know how serious this is?" He paused. "Some people with giardia are so weak they can't even stoop down to pick up a pin," he said emphatically. "Others have been hospitalized and some even have died." He just shook his head and insisted I complete an antibiotic prescription, despite the long delay.

The previous year in Hilton Head during the first 1988 USA Triathlon World Championship, a race entrepreneur by the name of Renee Roker had told us about a new triathlon in Saint Croix that would offer a purse to Age-Groupers as well as to the Pros who do these races for a living. This new race was called Beat the Beast, named after a horrendous hill with a 21-percent grade. I was intrigued with the idea of conquering this hill plus its many "relatives" on the bike course, so I traveled to Saint Croix to try it. While there, I had the privilege of staying with the West Indian Franciscan Sisters and was so impressed with the work they did to help those on the island that when I took first place in my age group, I left the money I had earned with these Sisters for their work.

In 1989, I Beat the Beast again the first Sunday in May, but in September Hurricane Hugo hit Saint Croix with such force, it devastated the island. I organized a volunteer group from Spokane to go there to help with reconstruction for a week, convincing American Airlines to give these volunteers free passage. Since then I have been to the island of Saint Croix for five more attempts to Beat the Beast and have always been impressed with the simplicity, hospitality, and resilience of these Crusians.

When hurricanes and other natural disasters hit, I often find myself trying to get inside the mind of God and ask. "What are you trying to show us?" I end up thinking that perhaps the Lord is giving us opportunities to display the good in our humanity when, all too frequently, wars and acts of terrorism demonstrate our inhumanity. These disasters are a chance to redeem ourselves by showing our capacity to love, to give of self and goods, and share in acts of compassion, kindness, and generosity.

14

Racing at Sixty

You are never too old for something new to happen.

THE YEAR AFTER I turned sixty, the Australians hosted the 1991 International Triathlon Union World Championship on the Gold Coast. The ITU course consisted of an Olympic distance of 1.5K swim, 40K bike, and 10k run, and I had some good competition. As we were standing on shore ready to go into the water, a woman who has regarded me as her nemesis because in many races she has been unable to beat me, said slyly, "I understand they have sharks out there." My reply was, "Oh, those poor things, how will they know which of these thrashing bodies to choose? They'll probably be freaked out!" After that there were no more attempts to psych me out although there had been several occasions previous to these big events when my bike had seemingly been sabotaged while in the transition area the night before.

I went on to win the gold with no shark attack. Six days later I set a new record in the Hawaiian Ironman, breaking this same woman's previous record for women aged sixty to sixty-four. The following year, in the 1992 event, I broke my own record for women in that age group with a time of 13:19:01, which remained unbroken for thirteen years.

But there were more heartbreaking challenges to face. In August 1991, I had received a phone call announcing that my mother had fallen and broken her hip. The accident had happened while she was playing Ping-Pong down in the basement with her great grandchild who was only two years old. Even at this early age he had the presence of mind to call upstairs to his mother, "Something wrong with Gammie. Something wrong with Gammie."

Just after I had returned from the 1992 Hawaiian Ironman in October, I received even worse news. My mother had suffered a stroke and was in intensive care. I flew to Saint Louis to be with her and went directly to the hospital, where one glance at my mother's ashen face made me think she could go any minute. I whispered in her ear, and she reached out her hand toward me. The nurses were surprised, because up to this point they had not gotten a response from her. My mother began mumbling. I tried to understand and gradually recognized a few words, but they were not in English. Then I turned to the nurse and said, "If we want to communicate with Mrs. Buder, we will have to learn French."

I tried responding to my mother in French, but she had never approved of my pronunciation. So I gave up on that and tried another approach. "Mommy, has this family got something against turning eighty-four, or what? Daddy died just four months shy of turning eighty-four, and his father died a few months short of that. Now you are only a month away from turning eighty-four. Are you going to set the record or not?"

When I finally got to my mother's home after this visit, I found to my amazement a French book wide open on the ottoman of the armchair in her sitting room. Apparently she had been studying her French before dressing to meet some friends who were picking her up for dinner. After waiting half an hour for her, they summoned her servant to inquire if she was almost ready. It was then that my mother was discovered on the bathroom floor unconscious.

Earlier that day she had been with her lawyer working on the disposition of her estate. This was always stressful for her. Now that she was incapacitated, her lawyer asked me to exercise power of attorney in these legal and financial matters. I think he mistook my years as a nun as evidence that I could be manipulated into signing anything he requested. He turned out to be untrustworthy, and I ended up hiring another attorney to protect my mother's interests.

The only thing that helped me through this emotional turmoil was my ability to go out for a run. It was therapy to run to and from the hospital, a round trip of six miles, to attend her every day. In the end, my mother rose to my challenge, surpassing the age of eighty-four. With round-the-clock care in her own home, she lived another eight years after her stroke, going to her reward at ninety-two on January 17, 2000. She evidently wanted to see what would happen in the year 2000.

During those eight years, I visited two or three times a year, and always at Christmas. I knew she was lonely and disappointed that she was not receiving more attention from her sons and their offspring, who lived much closer to her than I.

On one of these visits my oldest brother, with whom I had climbed Longs Peak and Hallett Peak, invited me to the Fairmount Park Racetrack in Illinois, not far from Saint Louis, to watch one of his horses race. We went down to the stables to see the horse before the race. Usually my brother liked to talk with his horses before they ran, but this time he stopped to talk to the trainer and ignored Royal Gold.

Observing that she'd been slighted, I sauntered over to chat with her instead. She looked bored or possibly hurt for being ignored, not at all spirited for the occasion. I touched her forehead, making the sign of the cross, telling her how nice it would be for her to perform a feat that would please her owner. It would make her much more valuable if he decided to sell her and give her another happy home. She became more attentive as I prayed over her.

Then I rejoined my sister-in-law up in the bleachers, where we had a good view of the race on the TV monitor, while my brother went over to the betting booth. In the first quarter of the race, my brother's horse was dead last. Before long, she began to move up to the middle. When the horses rounded the last turn she was outside in sixth place. Once on the straightaway, she took over the lead and bolted over the finish in first place.

My brother won a measly seventy-five dollars from his bet. Thrusting the rolled-up bills in my face, he inquired, "What did you say to her?" My response, "That's between her and me," left him mystified. The crowd was stunned by Royal Gold's performance.

*   *   *

During my travels going from competition to competition, I often was in need of angelic assistance. As if the challenge of the event itself weren't enough, I could almost always count on my travels lending some hair-raising excitement. In 1994, I traveled to Tasmania for the International Duathlon World Champion-ship and was on a flight over to Wellington, New Zealand, for the International Triathlon Union World Championship the fol-lowing week. High winds forced our flight to divert to Auckland, where we deplaned and spent three hours, from one thirty to four thirty in the morning, as airport captives until we were sum-moned to reboard. Once we were in the air, it was still dark, and the weather below us looked menacing. The beginning of the descent into Wellington was like riding a bucking bronco. Then the pilot announced that we were being diverted—again!—this time to Christchurch. We seemed to be getting a free air tour of New Zealand from the North to South islands.

The ocean depths below did not look the least bit inviting, especially after the pilot announced we had developed a "techni-cal problem." This happened shortly after I noticed a flash of light and smelled something burning. As I was pondering the meaning of this, the pilot made another announcement, prepar-ing us for the fact that we might need to make an "abnormal landing" because one of the flaps on the right wing would not release. I tried to see what was happening from my window seat over the right-hand wing, but could detect nothing only that this is where I had noticed the flash.

As I contemplated a possible cold water landing, I complained, "Lord, my wet suit is in the belly of the plane—a lot of good it will do me. This whole situation is looking rather dismal. Time for You to act. Why not rally all the guardian angels aboard and have them flap their wings to keep this craft afloat?" I did not mean on the water but in the air!

Praying earnestly and making periodic checks out the window, I noticed that the flap farthest out on the wing's tip that had not released was beginning to flutter. I hoped that was enough to do the trick and I kept praying. Then came the descent into Christchurch. The landing was surprisingly smooth, and passengers jumped up from their seats into the aisle before the plane came to a halt, eager to deplane. I stayed put, knowing how long it takes to open doors. Because I was on the opposite side, I had not spotted the fire brigade awaiting us on the tarmac. Once the news trickled down to me, I was out of my seat in a hurry. It took a while before I managed to re-claim my bike and re-book yet another flight back to Wellington.

By the time I got there, I was twelve hours behind schedule and grateful the race was not the following day. The winds had stirred the waters into white caps, and there were small-craft warnings. I used the time I had to chance a swim in the harbor. It felt like being in a washing machine on the cold cycle. I swam the whole course having to stop every twenty strokes to bail out my goggles and open my eyes just to see if I was still in the harbor or if I had been washed out to sea.

On race day, the sky was gray and windy, the water cold and choppy. Before the start, while leaving the bike transition area, a fellow racer was frantically asking if anyone had a spray can of Wesson oil. She got an empty stare from me. I thought, "What for?" A good hour later, I knew the answer. It took me as long to pry off my wet suit with numb hands as it did to swim the course—or so it seemed. Smearing myself with some sort of oil beforehand would have helped.

Another lesson learned. By now I'd come to expect the unexpected.

In 1995, I moved into a new age group, for women sixty-five to sixty-nine. My goal was to win this age group in order to open it for women in the Hawaiian Ironman. This put me in direct competition with the same woman who had tried to psych me out about the possibility of sharks in a previous World Championship race. Her heart was also set on the gold. On at least four occasions, my bike had been tampered with, but only in those events where she too was competing. It seemed as if she wanted to win at any cost. Up to this point I had never carried a bike pump, tools, or spare tires. This year, however, given the stakes, I had a hunch I should be prepared.

I was riding a Litespeed bike given me by a dealer from Suburban Machinery in Detroit. It was going to be the maiden voyage for the new wheels donated by Zipp. I had gone only about thirteen miles on the bike course when I felt a strange shifting in the rear of my bike. At first I attributed this odd sensation to the new tires but since I had no previous experience with them, I figured I had better check it out. I rolled on a bit farther beyond the second aid station when I noticed two men watching from the hillside. Dismounting, I yelled to them, "Can you tell if I have a flat?" They nodded. "Yes, Ma'am, you do."

"Do you know how to fix it?"

They came down to me, asking whether I wanted a quick fix or a thorough fix.

"How about both?"

When I unzipped the saddle pack to yank out the spare, two pennies dropped out. How did those get here? Maybe these guys are pennies from heaven! The task was done before I knew it. Good thing I had carried a spare. The guys even congratulated me on having a good pump.

By the end of the race, I had weaseled into first place despite the tire problem. Nevertheless, I thanked the Lord for sending His angels. When I took the tire to the bike shop they said the damage was very puzzling. The tire had been scraped along the sidewall instead of at the point of contact with the road. Suspecting that it was sabotaged in the transition area after we checked in our bikes the night before, I sent the tire back to Continental manufacturers to inquire if they could determine whether the damage to the tire had happened because of the flat during the race or if it had happened beforehand. They had no comment but graciously provided me with a new tire, saving me sixty dollars. Manufacturers can be angels, too!

15

Juggling Acts

Being a nun is a life, not a lifestyle.

"Sorry I can't talk any longer now, I have to go to jail." Because of my regular jail ministry, I have sometimes had to interrupt a conversation to make this remark. This leaves the other person stunned, if they are not acquainted with what I do. After I joined the Sisters for Christian Community, I began to work with women in the Spokane County Jail. I have continued that work to this day, and it's one of the most rewarding things I do.

Women in jail are either hungry for God and find God while they are there, or could care less about Him and concentrate only on the day and the way they can return to their pastimes. On the other hand, for those who are open to repentance it's amazing what happens when they are taken from the distractions of the world. Some come into contact with a Source that is more powerful than anything they have ever experienced before and are overwhelmingly responsive.

I try to impress on those I visit, especially those who feel guilt or are down on themselves, that they do God a disservice by not acknowledging that His loving mercy is far greater than any offense they may have committed. I tell them, "Rather than falling to pieces, make peace." The motto of the founders of my former order, the Sisters of the Good Shepherd, was "One soul is worth more than a world." I really believe if I am able to touch just one person, it is worth the effort of my continuous visits. That's what Jesus did. He had crowds around him all the time, but even the least person mattered. Sometimes just being present to someone and giving them your ear is healing in itself.

These women in jail usually have no one but each other to share their concerns, and that's not always helpful. So when someone like me comes from the outside, and comes back again and again, they notice and are grateful. I am very humbled when they make this observation and thank me for coming.

On occasion I have even heard from some of the girls I worked with during my early days at the Sisters of the Good Shepherd. After my picture appeared in a newspaper in connection with a running event, I received a letter from one of the young women who had been a ward of the court and was one of the girls I had worked with twenty-seven years before. "Thank you for all you were and all you gave to me, gave to us, so very long ago," she wrote. "The last time I saw you, you were dressed in black and white from the top of your head to the tips of your toes. I never saw more of you than your elegant hands and your strong but poetic face. What a shock to see you in shorts and T-shirt! I'm not even sure I am writing to the right person."

More recently, when I was on a street corner in Spokane waiting for the signal to change, a gal stopped me and asked if I'd ever visited jail. I said, "That's where I'm coming from now," I said. "Are you Sister Madonna by any chance?" I nodded yes.

"I can't tell you how much you helped me while I was there," she told me. "Now I have a new grandson and I've been clean ever since."

This same day, as I was coming from my jail visit, another woman stopped me and said practically the same thing. I thought, "Oh my gosh, Lord, this is really confirmation that what I am doing is what you want. It is obvious that there is a need for this kind of work."

Then there was a Jewish woman who had been very regular in attending the prayer sessions during these visits. After two years in the county jail, she was sentenced to the Washington State Corrections Center, on the other side of the state from Spokane. One day I happened to be in the vicinity of that prison so I decided to visit her. It was hard enough getting inside through the heavy security but it was worse getting out.

Once outside, I started running back the way I'd come, my natural way of getting places. As I was loping along, I heard shouts. "Stop! Stop or I'll shoot!" This last remark brought me to an abrupt stop. When confronted I explained that I was a Catholic Sister and had just been in prison visiting one of the inmates. Skeptical, the armed guard said, "Follow me." Back to prison I went. Once they checked out my story, I was released, but with the solemn warning not to run while on the premises. On my next visit I was careful to restrain my gait.

* * *

Juggling jail isn't the only thing that requires flexibility. Triathlons have provided me occasions to minister to others as well. I never consciously set out to do this. It just happens. People have bared their souls to me during marathons especially. It is as if the talking takes away the burden of miles as well as the troubles they are bearing. When I minister to them I no longer care about the race, but about the people who have reached out to me. Also I frequently bless people along the way and get blessings in return.

During races, it's challenging enough to keep body and soul together across the required distances, but there's always another element—the weather, whether it's torrential rains, strong winds, or unrelenting heat. When I arrived in Florida in mid-May 1996 for the Gulf Coast Half Ironman Triathlon, I drove up with a friend from St. Petersburg to Panama City Beach, an eight-hour drive that landed us there in the dark so we were totally unaware of what the ocean was doing.

We awoke the next morning to find the red flags flying, the beach barren of people, even seagulls, and sand blowing everywhere. Going through the Expo area, I noticed four of the race staff mulling over a huge map. When I asked what they were doing, they said they were trying to redesign the course into a duathlon and were trying to figure out how long to make the run to replace the 1.2-mile swim.

My response was, "Remember, the night is twelve hours long." They glanced at each other quizzically, as if to say, "She has a point." I sauntered on.

That evening, when we gathered with the Race Director for the orientation meeting, I decided to sit right up under the platform so I could hear his solemn pronouncement about what would take place the next day. Instead, what I heard was, "Is

Sister Madonna here?" I waved my hand in front of him. "Right here below you!"

"Will you please come up to the stage?" he asked. "Uh-oh," I said to myself. I knew he wanted me to give the invocation before the race in the morning. I was prepared for that, but now he was probably expecting me to pray this weather away.

I thought to myself, "O God, it doesn't seem proper for me to tell You what to do about your own Creation. Please give me the right words to say." It was then that I got an inspiration. Knowing that God promised, "Where two or three are gathered together, there I am in their midst," I addressed those assembled as a community of spirits with a common cause to present.

"Let us pray that our spirits be filled with faith and confidence in a loving Father who wants the best for His children," I prayed. As I continued, I was aware that the tenseness was beginning to subside and the audience of athletes was beginning to relax. Consequently the race director said that the final decision about the swim would not be made until the next morning.

I woke up early and had started down the boardwalk for the beach when I saw one of the staff coming toward me from the opposite direction. "Well, Sister, what do you think?" The wind had abated during the night and the ocean was like glass. I glanced up at the white flag and affirmed, "Let's go for it!"

During the race, all was placid. God seemingly allowed us to slip through the cracks, because the following morning at the Awards breakfast on the beach it was all we could do to hold on to our paper plates and the morsels on top of them. We had plenty of sand for seasoning.

The next year, one of our renowned competitors, Judith Flannery, had been killed before the race in a freakish accident with an oncoming car when she was out training on her bike with two companions. Again I was asked to give the invocation before the race. I dedicated the race in her memory and called on the Master of the wind and the waves to clear our way. After the race, several people came up to me and said, "Thank you for your prayer, Sister. It brought tears to my eyes."

To me, faith is the muscle of our being. When I awake in the morning, life is always a new beginning, a fresh start, and I ask, "Okay, God, what is on the agenda for today?" then run off to Mass. This prepares me for whatever unravels during the day.

16

Overcoming the Odds

*Acceptance is the key to a balanced life
with no regrets.*

EUROPEAN COURSES ARE notoriously challenging. I experienced that first in August 1998 during the International Triathlon Union World Duathlon Championship, held in Saint Wendel, Germany, and a week later in Lausanne, Switzerland, at the ITU World Championship Triathlon. These Europeans are sadistic and seem to compete with each other to see who can make the courses the most formidable.

The timing was bad for me because I was coping with a lingering leg injury inflicted the month before. I had been coming home from a long training ride, and at a stop sign I attempted to make a wide turn to get around the car that had stopped. Suddenly the bike spun out from under me, and I landed with a big thud on my right buttock. I hobbled the remaining three-tenths of a mile home, but my leg was so painful the next day, which happened to be the Fourth of July, that a friend had to take me to the emergency room. The doctors found no fracture in my leg, so I thought, "Okay, I guess we just keep on going, pain or no pain." But the swelling didn't subside much, and the accident probably left me with a pinched nerve in that area, which ran down my entire leg.

Despite this obstacle, I went on to Ohio and did the Sylvania Triathlon there, although I had considerable difficulty running. I had to count my running steps and when I reached thirty, stopped to walk. These repeats got me to the finish line. From there, I caught a flight to Germany for the International Triathlon Union World Duathlon Championship. Sitting for hours on that long flight did not help.

The run portion of the Saint Wendel's course was partly off road through a forest going uphill. Yep, those Europeans! I just walked and fudged through the best I could, and ended up bringing home the gold in my age group for Team USA. I must have been the only contender in my age group! European women at this age didn't seem interested in these activities.

A week later a German friend and I drove on to Lausanne. The food in that part of the world was so expensive that I ate very sparingly. When it was time for the start of the ITU World Championship Triathlon in Lausanne, the water in Lake Geneva was cold, and I had nothing but a sleeveless wet suit. By the time I got out of the water it took me eight minutes to gain the use of my hands in order to pull on my cycling jersey and shorts.

When I got on the bike, I created my own breeze, which chilled me even more. One hill went straight up after an abrupt right-angle turn. There was no time to gain momentum, and my energy had already been sapped from partial hypothermia so I had to dismount. The run also included a long extension over cobblestone streets. My teeth rattled so hard I thought I'd lose my gold fillings. I had not been able to train adequately for the run because of my injured leg. It took everything I had to push myself through the pain of running.

At the finish line, a German newscaster thrust a microphone in my face. I hadn't gotten through the first sentence when all of a sudden I couldn't talk. Startled, he took me to the medical tent where I lay on a cot for quite a while before I was told I was having an asthma attack. But I had never had asthma, so I wondered if the sheer stress on my body had caused the disruptive breathing. I had used every ounce of my energy to get through the run with my lame leg. I was still wearing my wet swimsuit, so they wrapped me in a space blanket while I waited for a massage to help my circulation. But waiting motionless made me cold and jump-started my erratic breathing all over again. An ambulance was summoned.

An American family with a little girl saw me waiting in a wheelchair, and the father said, "Sister, what's the matter with you?" I said, "Nothing, but they want to take me to the hospital. Please tell your little daughter to unfasten the belt on this wheelchair so I can escape." Just then the ambulance arrived. "Oops! Too late," I muttered.

At the hospital, the attendants threw this lovely down comforter over me. I sighed, "Oh body, lay me down. I don't care if I ever wake up again." I did drop off to sleep before they got around to me. I told them I really needed something to eat, that I hadn't had anything since early morning. They gave me the best meal I had had since I arrived in Switzerland, which helped to stabilize me. They never did figure out what was wrong so they released me. Maybe the combination of the pollution in the cities, not getting enough to eat, and the physical exertion and pushing through the pain on the run is what had done me in.

When I was discharged, I had no money, no change of clothing, and had to catch a bus to get back to the race site. I am not sure how I talked myself onto the bus, but the driver dropped me off where I knew I could meet up with my fellow citizens from Team USA.

From Munich I returned to Saint Louis to visit my mother and do the Lake Saint Louis Triathlon. It was now the second month since the accident, and my leg was feeling no better. That long flight from Munich to Saint Louis slowed the healing too. The run was so painful that I actually burst into tears when I got to the finish line. The following week I participated in a duathlon held in Grand Prairie, Texas, with my leg still not functioning well. It is a mystery to me how I managed to get first place in all of these races, except in Switzerland where I came in second. Now it was September, and I had completed six races with the injured leg.

When it was time for the monstrous Hawaiian Ironman, scheduled for October 3, the injury was still plaguing me. Before the race began, one of the pros, Wendy Ingraham, asked me for a blessing: "Sister, do you have a moment to pray for me as I go into this race?" I asked whether she was frightened or anxious, and she said she was both. So I spontaneously put my hands on her head and the words just poured out that the Lord give her the strength and the wisdom to race her own race and not to worry about the competition, but to listen to her inner strength, and let it flow.

Wendy came out of the swim in first place, proceeded to remain in first for the entire bike ride, and was still in the lead with only nine miles to go in the run. Suddenly she bonked, having run out of fuel from not hydrating sufficiently. Some of her competitors began to pass her. When she neared the finish line, one of the women who had passed her, Sian Welsh, was on four legs crawling toward the finish. At that point Wendy's legs got wobbly too and she fell to the ground. Noticing that Sian was crawling, Wendy decided to do the same, so they had a crawling race to the finish. Wendy got her hand over the finish line first and ended up in third place just in front of Sian. They were both promptly hauled to the medical tent for an IV.

As for me, I was totally unaware of this scene that had preceded me. It was all I could do to keep limping to the finish. All I had to do was cross the finish line to grab first place in the women's 65–69 category, and Wendy was there to assist me. What a delight to have her at my side! It was this welcoming presence that made me feel "I'm home at last."

When I look back on all this, I realize that athletes who do these events are like people possessed. It's hard to realize this when you are actually doing it and so intent to reach the finish line. You are simply in survival mode even if it means crawling over the finish line. How did I ever do these six races in such pain and manage to compete in three major championships, including the Hawaiian Ironman, with a bum leg? All I can say is, "Lord, without your providing me with the will to endure, I could not have done it."

*   *   *

It had been my habit to visit my mother in Saint Louis over Christmas. It was now eight years since her stroke, and I spent most of the time reading her expressions since speech came with difficulty due to her aphasia. It was soon to be the last night of 1999, and I was returning home on New Year's Eve day uncertain as to what would happen when 2000 rolled around. She had had a lot of exertion during the day when surprised by a visit from one of her granddaughter's entire family. As I was tucking her in, she turned to me and said very clearly, "I want to go home."

"Mommy, you are in your comfortable home, in your cozy little bed, ready to go to sleep now," I countered. She still seemed agitated, as if I hadn't gotten the message, so I took a leap of faith and said, "But—if you mean you want to go home to God, you are more than ready. Just call on Saint Peter, so he can swing those pearly gates open wide to receive you." I sensed her relaxing, so I went on to say, "If this is what you really want, you have my permission to go." She relaxed. I had understood.

By morning she seemed stronger. Feeling that she was stable, I departed for Spokane as planned. I had always asked God to let me be present when she breathed her last. However, after I had been home in Spokane for seventeen days, I was awakened by a call from my mother's nurse in Saint Louis informing me my mother had gone "home" at seven o'clock that morning. I was angry at first that she hadn't cooperated with my desire to be present with her when she breathed her last, but soon realized it was typical of her thoughtfulness, by trying to preserve me from further stress. After all, I had given her permission to "go home," so the choice was up to her.

They say that death often occurs in threes. My mother's yard man was next, and then came one completely unexpected loss. I was returning from the International Assembly of the Sisters for Christian Community in San Diego when I learned my flight was delayed, making for a tight connection in Oakland on my way back to Spokane. As we deplaned in Oakland, the flight attendant warned us to hurry. In my haste, I shot beyond the concourse where my final flight was to take off. All of a sudden a man appeared on my left with a pleasant expression, wearing a Hawaiian shirt with my mother's favorite colors, dusty pink and robin's egg blue. He said, "If you are going to Spokane, you have to turn around and take the concourse just behind you, but you must hurry." I thought to myself, "How could he know where I was headed?" Nor did I remember seeing him on my plane to Oakland. Besides, not everyone on my plane was transfering to Spokane.

When I got to the numbered gate, there were two entries with the same number, but one was marked A and one B. I lined up with a woman who had a child with her. I asked her how come she wasn't boarding early. She said, "This isn't my flight, it's the other one." I was puzzled. "What other one?"

Just at that moment, the man in the Hawaiian shirt reappeared and said, "Go immediately to this gate," pointing to B. Without questioning, I did as I was told. Once I settled into my seat, I wondered about the urgency that required an "angel escort." The take off was immediate and I sighed with relief. "Lord, it's a miracle I'm even on this flight!"

By the time I reached home, I had a number of phone messages. One was from my brother in Denver, announcing that his oldest son had been in a serious motorcycle accident and was in intensive care. He had been in a coma for six days now and wasn't expected to live. A day later my brother called to inform me that Alex had died. Now I knew why it had been so important that I make the right flight back to Spokane, and why I had received some angelic assistance. Had I arrived a day later, I would not have been able to make arrangements to go to the funeral. Now I just had enough time to arrange a bereavement flight to Denver so I could be present for my nephew's funeral service and help console the family.

The year 2000 was filled with loss. My mother died in January, I lost my nephew in August, and I could have lost my own life in October during the Hawaiian Ironman when my bike and body were airborne and deposited on the road. Up to this point I had already completed eleven triathlons and three duathlons. That's fourteen major events from April to September, and my heart wasn't in any of them because I was still suffering from the loss of my mother.

Whether because of the losses or in spite of them, I kept pushing on. The 2000 International Triathlon Union World Championship was hosted in April by the Aussies in Perth. I arrived before the race and was staying with some Sisters of the Presentation, trying to get in a little pre-race training. I found a cove not too far away where I thought I might be able to swim. I had not stroked more than one hundred yards when I realized I was surrounded by blue bottles, a type of jellyfish often found in Australian waters. Not knowing whether or not they were lethal, I tried to avoid swimming into them, but it was like swimming through an obstacle course. Later in the week, I decided to train in the body of water we were actually going to swim in. Guess what? More jellyfish! I was swimming without a wet suit, and by this time I was getting used to their sleazy feel. They turned out to be the least of my problems.

It wasn't until I had gotten to the finish and an Australian reporter was attempting to interview me regarding my win that I noticed something strange about my left hand. When I held out my fingers the middle one seemed to dangle and was quite limp. I remembered having had more than the usual difficulty that day removing my wet suit in transition after the swim, eager to get out onto the bike course as quickly as possible. I excused myself to the reporter, saying, "I think I better find the medical tent, if you don't mind." We both set out to find it. All they could do for my floppy finger was to bind it until it was sticking out straight. I asked, "Don't you happen to have a tongue depressor?" They apologized, saying, "No we don't, but just binding it will keep your finger stiff until you get to a doctor."

A couple of days later I boarded a plane for California, where I was planning to do the Wildflower Triathlon, a Half Ironman event at Lake San Antonio. I asked the flight attendant for a couple of Band-Aids and some stirrers usually used for drinks, and proceeded to construct my own splint.

This was my first Wildflower event. My friend Bobbi Pollock picked me up at the airport and drove me over the bike course on her way home, where she had invited me to stay. When I saw how technically challenging the course was, I began to wonder how I would be able to shift my bicycle gears with my finger sticking straight out. This was a week after the World Championship in Australia, and I still hadn't seen a doctor. But once the event was underway I had other things to concentrate on. It was such a challenging course, I totally forgot about my finger and ended up winning my age group.

Two weeks later, my doctor at home said I had a torn ligament, which only time could heal. This meant I would also do the Canadian Ironman in August with extended finger. Apparently, in my haste to remove my wet suit in Perth, I had put too much stress on that finger. By October, when the 2000 Hawaiian Ironman took place, my finger had healed, but unbenownst to me I was headed for a whole new set of injuries there. That airborne experience could have resulted in me permanently flapping my wings had it not been for some greater force at work. My fall seemed cushioned by a fleet of angels. I was certain both my mother and my nephew were included in their company.

17

In My Seventies

Opposition is really a backhanded compliment. It indicates you are worth opposing and is an invitation to persevere.

BY THE 2001 season I was seventy-one and ready again for Kona. With God's help, I healed quickly from the airborne accident the year before. After getting trashed on my bike like that, I didn't want others to think the Ironman could end someone's racing days so I decided to be a "comeback kid."

But September 11 came, and it changed the meaning of the race for all of us. My plan was to persuade the race committee that they should turn the event into a memorial for those who had died in the terrorist attack. We encouraged fellow triathletes to carry U.S. flags on their bikes. I wrote an invocation, which the staff could use, and the race committee gave out embroidered flag patches that we could sew onto our attire. I've kept mine on ever since.

Several months after I finished the 2001 Hawaiian Ironman,

I learned I had been chosen by the Ironman Committee to receive the Iron Spirit Award. This would be given at the *Competitor* Magazine Awards Banquet in California in February. When Lew Friedland informed me of the nomination via a long-distance call from the World Triathlon Corporation (WTC) headquarters in Florida, I nearly fell off the stool on which I was perched. Nearly in tears, I stammered a weak, "Who? Me?" but accepted the invitation for the presentation. I was still mourning the loss of my mother, and this was a boost to my spirits.

At seventy-two, when I had been racing in the seventy to seventy-five age group for a couple of years, I set my sights on breaking my former record in the 2002 Ironman Canada. I had a new bike, and I was right on target until I got out on the run and my stomach shut down. I began to suffer from nausea, unable to eat anything, which led to weakness and exhaustion. I was only a third of the way through the run when I deposited my cookies along the run course. From then on my stomach wouldn't allow me to take anything in, not even water. It was humiliating and reduced my finish time considerably. Still I did finish and was amazed to find I had even beaten the men in my age group.

Afterward, the announcer Steve King, who does his homework like no one else, said publicly that they were hoping that I would come back the next year. I assured him that, against my better judgment, I had indeed signed up for the 2003 Canadian Ironman. I figured I would just bring some Tums along and beat this stomach issue.

But before then, I began hatching a plan. There were no ultradistance races just for women, so I started dreaming about putting one together. I knew I'd have to be careful about the

title—I couldn't call it Ironwoman, because the Ironman organizers are so guarded about the Ironman signature.

At first I thought of calling it the Ironmaiden Race, but
then a friend told me what "iron maidens" were in Germany. It
was actually a term for prostitutes who dressed in black leather
and carried whips. I didn't want to be associated with that, so I
thought, well, how about Molten Maidens? Finally I decided to
call my event Maidens of Mettle, MOM Triathlon for short.

I thought it would be nice to put this sport back where it was in
the beginning—a race for the pure joy of competing. In the years
since I had been competing, membership in the USA Triathlon
organization had been doubling every couple of years and races
were multiplying across the world. When events used to dovetail
each other nicely, now there are so many on the same date, you
have to pick and choose carefully. Once triathlons had been included in the 2000 Olympic Games in Sydney, Australia, they had
gained worldwide attention and participation had been driven up
even further. Of course, all kinds of new commercial enterprises
started up from sponsorship, to equipment manufacturers, to
clothing designers, all of course with dollar signs attached.

This race I envisioned would be a contemplative experience,
out in the desert portion of Washington State where there are
no crowds, just God's primitive landscape. I'd keep everything as
simple as possible. I would not charge a hefty entry fee, just one
hundred dollars to cover organizational expenses. Maybe I could
get a breast cancer organization to be a beneficiary, and people
could donate whatever they could, from a penny multiplied by
a thousand times if they so wished. There would be a finisher's
medal, but no purse for winners, which is why most Professionals

race. I would invite the Pros to join the age group divisions just for pure enjoyment.

On the drive back from Canada, daydreaming about all this, I stopped at the Grand Coulee Dam where I was routed back to Spokane. I realized I'd found the ideal spot. Within the year, I took several trips back to that area with friends to decide where the elements of a race might be laid out. It culminated in my meeting with the Grand Coulee Chamber of Commerce in August of 2003. They seemed enthusiastic, but their resources were limited. So, I began reaching out to others. At the Lake Stevens Triathlon in Washington State in September 2003, I had met one of the race marshals, who seemed enthusiastic when he overheard me talking about my idea for Maidens of Mettle and had offered his assistance. I was already in the process of laying the groundwork when he bounced on the scene. I had made the necessary contacts, set the course, inquired about permits, and even obtained permission to take the bikes over Grand Coulee Dam, barring an Orange Alert.

His interest seemed genuine so I made arrangements to show him the bike course, swim course, and a portion of the run course. I even gave him names of some key contacts. This was shortly before I was to depart for a two-month race circuit, beginning with the Hawaiian Ironman in October and concluding with the ITU World Championship in Queenstown, New Zealand, in December. His enthusiasm was running high, and he pressed me to enlist him in service before I left. I said further plans would have to be put on hold until I returned in January.

To my amazement, when I returned, I found that he had used the months I'd been gone to organize his own race, using all the information I had shared with him in good faith. What would have

been Maidens of Mettle, he stamped as his own, allowing men
to participate, calling it by another name, and altering the course.

I had to explain to all those who had supported me that these
changes had happened without my knowledge, and that I had
never intended to abandon Maidens of Mettle. I felt betrayed at
the time, but after I mulled it over, I realized that women were
gradually coming into their own in the long-distance events,
gaining in confidence, and did not need their own race, so I decided to lay my dream to rest.

Normally, for most years my race season would go from spring
to fall, leaving me three months to hibernate. But in 2003, the
ITU World Championship was being held in Queenstown, New
Zealand, in December, and I wanted to be part of it, even though
events late in the season when Spokane's wintry weather had
settled in always posed a challenge for training outdoors. Therefore I went from the Hawaiian Ironman in October to Tasmania to be with a friend through November to get acclimated for
the competition in Queenstown. This was the first time I had
been to that southern region of New Zealand, with its lakes, rug-
ged hillsides covered in brilliant yellow Scotch broom, and high
peaks capped with snow.

Three days before the triathlon, I decided to enter the
Aquathon, a swim-run combination. This took place in Lake
Wakatipu, close to town. It was beautiful but frigid. I didn't have
a neoprene beanie to keep my head warm, so I donned three
swim caps. When I jumped into the water it took my breath
away. I thought, "Oh, God, how am I going to endure this for
twenty-plus minutes?" I was already in and there was nothing I

could do except start moving my limbs. As I looked down at the bottom, I realized I had never seen such clear water. Every multicolored stone was visible. I said, "Lord, let me concentrate on the clarity and beauty of these waters rather than the coldness."

Somehow I got through the swim and was able to disentangle myself from my wet suit with frozen hands so as to set out on the run. It was hard to gain any momentum and I wasn't able to do much more than a jog pace, but I finished. I was sapped of energy for the next several days. All of a sudden it dawned on me! I was probably suffering from mild hypothermia. The water, I learned later, had been 54 degrees. I wasn't sure my energy would return in time for the big race. Fortunately, the bike course in that race was filled with hills that gave me the opportunity to work off the chill from the choppy swim, only two degrees warmer than in the previous lake. Sustained winds battered us for the length of the .9 mile (1.5K) swim.

When I toed the finish line, Les McDonald, the Canadian who had masterminded the ITU World Championships, the first being in Avignon in 1989, approached me. He said I should go to the Portuguese Island of Madeira the following year for the 2004 ITU World Championship being held there, the distance being 1.5K swim, 40K bike, 10K run, and forget about these long Ironman distances. He promised to make arrangements with the race director so I would have a place to stay. I had more than a few miles of living to do before I got to Portugal nine months later with a few more adventures thrown in.

My 2004 schedule began with Saint Anthony's Triathlon in Saint Petersburg, Florida, on April 25. After that, I was to fly to

New York at the request of the owner of the Swim, Bike, Run Triathlon shop centrally located in New York City. He had invited me to give a presentation. The person assigned to pick me up at the airport asked the owner if he also wanted him available for my return the next day, but arrangements to pick me up were not firmly established. This made me uneasy since I had an international flight to board for Madeira where the ITO World Championship was to be held. I knew I had to be at the airport early. When no one showed up at the hotel to pick me up, I hiked to the bike shop. It was Sunday, but fortunately the owner was there. He ordered a cab, but I arrived at the airport too late to get my bike aboard the international flight. This blunder delayed me a whole day. I was frantic. The airline supervisor took pity on me and offered a hotel waiver. But this meant I had to haul my bike and baggage single-handedly to catch a monorail for the hotel, which was some distance from the airport. There was scarcely anyone left in the airport where I was preparing to bed down. I was in dismay, when a worker offered to help me get my bike into the elevator. I told him of my dilemma. He got on his cell phone and managed to get me a hotel closer to the airport that would accept my voucher. Another angel to ease my distress!

My first day in Madeira I was eager to get out to explore the magic of my surroundings. I roamed through cobblestone streets, past stone buildings, and down narrow little alleys. Red tile roofs glistened in the sun. The houses were on terraced slopes. There was nothing level on the island. Then I decided to venture out to the breakwater to get a view of the whole city. It was absolutely intriguing, and as I drank in the beauty of these tiered homes peppering the mountainside, I didn't notice an iron ring, used to secure boats, at my feet until I tripped over it, falling hard on both knees. I had the feeling my right knee was wrenched. There I was on all fours with no one to help around! After the shock of the fall I managed to swivel around on my posterior and ease myself up, first drawing the wounded knee to my chest to snap it back into place. I was a bloody mess so I hobbled to the first hotel I came across, went into the lobby as if I belonged, and asked for an ice pack. Not wanting to bloody the sitting area, I went outside and sat down on the cement steps to apply the ice. Rivulets of pink liquid dripped to the cobblestone street. It took a while before I could get back to my original hotel without leaving a bloody trail.

This was just three days before the race. I still needed to unpack my bike, put it together, and test it. We had been cautioned, however, not to go out on the streets to train because the traffic was too thick and the streets too narrow. No matter which direction I looked there was a hill. But I needed to know if I could mount a hill on my bike with my injured knee. I dared the traffic and got out on the road to go several miles up a hill that seemed to take forever to plateau. That done, I said, "Enough is enough," somewhat assured that my knee could take the pressure and that the bike was working.

The race course led us through tunnels at least seven times on a highway that ribboned around the island. The darkened tunnels made it very difficult to decide whether to wear sunglasses or not. Some of the tunnels were a mile long, so I decided to forgo sunglasses. On one horrendous hill, I couldn't get my bike to shift down to the lowest gear so was forced to dismount and walk it up. Somehow I made it through the bike course and squeaked through the run to nab the Gold in my age group for Team USA. Most probably I was the only contestant my age.

At 14 months, with my younger brother and mother.

At 14 months, running toward my father.

Training my cocker spaniel, Winkie, whom I received on my twelfth birthday. She was eight weeks old.

At 16, with Winkie. *Photo by Jules Pierlow*

Posing for the cover of an equestrian magazine, with my horse, Wally Highland. I was given the horse on my sixteenth birthday.

At age 20, posing with another horse. Wally Highland had recently died. *From the collections of the St. Louis Mercantile Library at the University of Missouri-St. Louis*

Playing the lead role of Grazia in Alberto Casella's *Death Takes a Holiday* at age 23. I entered the convent three weeks later.

Shortly after taking my final vows as a Sister of the Good Shepherd in Angers, France, December 8, 1956.

Graduating from Arizona State University, spring of 1968, with a master in counseling and a master in educational psychology. *Photo by Charles R. Conley, Photographer*

Winning the 65–69 women's age group at the 1999 Hawaiian Ironman at age 69. *Photo by Ironman*

In the trophy room at home posing for the spring 2005 issue of *Geezerjock* magazine, right before my seventy-fifth birthday. *Photo by J. Craig Sweat*

Ascending Richter Pass during the 2009 Canadian Ironman at age 79.
Photo by Action Sports International, www.asiphoto.com

*   *   *

Before I knew it, I had outgrown another age group. With the 2005 Canadian Ironman coming up on August 28, my goal was to open up a new age group for women seventy-five to seventy-nine, a group that had never before existed at an Ironman distance of 2.4-mile swim, 112-mile bike, and 26.2-mile run.

All went well during the swim and bike portions in Penticton, but well into the run, I found myself walking alone in the dark with eight miles still to go. My body was crying out, "I want to go home! I want a bed! I have had enough of all this! I have nothing more to prove! Nobody will care whether or not I finish anyway!" Then came a contrasting thought. "Oh no you don't! You started this thing and no one else is going to finish it but you. You are obligated to open this new age group for women." That word *obligated* stuck with me and kept me moving toward the finish line. "You are obligated. . . . You are obligated. . . ." resonated with each step I took and became my mantra.

With scarcely a mile and a half to go, my stomach was in an uproar. I was clinging to a lamp post heaving the little I had left in my stomach when an ambulance came by. The driver wanted to scoop me up, but I waved him on. I was not about to take the suggestion.

When I closed in on the finish line, I could hear the crowds. Steve King was the announcer and had done a good job of keeping the crowd fired up. He was yelling at the top of his voice, "Ladies and gentlemen, you are witnessing history in the making. Sister Madonna has just opened a new age group and set a fourth age-group record!" I crossed the finish line in 16:46:21 and literally fell into the arms of the race director, who had waited for me close to midnight, the bewitching hour. As she was putting the finishing medal over my neck, she said, "You are a pioneer." Just hearing this made me think it was worth the effort after all. I had fulfilled my "obligation."

I knew I was the oldest woman to finish an Ironman, but it wasn't until four months later when I was thinking back over the event that I realized, "Hey, there have been no men any older than you who have actually finished the race. This makes you the oldest finisher ever." That realization came as a shock, and I said, "Lord, how did this ever happen that I should be doing this at this ripe old age?" The following year, two men competed in the 75–79 age group, but only one finished. By now there are several men who have crawled out of the woodwork to join the ranks of 75-plus elders.

I had yet the Hawaiian Ironman to do in less than two months with the same goal in mind. For some reason, this went a bit easier for me, as my stomach maintained better on the run. Amazingly, I was able to open the 75–79 age group with a finishing time of 15:54:15. While my long-standing record for women 60–64, which I had held for thirteen years, and my eleven-year record for 65–69 were being broken during this same race, I was happy now to set the record for yet a new age group of 75–79 for women.

Now the question was, "When will we get an eighty-year-old female finisher?"

On September 1, a week after the Canadian Ironman, I did the Titanium Man in Richmond, Washington. This was only an Olympic distance—1.5K swim, 40K bike, and a 10K run—but still, I was amazed at my time of 3:01:52, which was better than some of my previous years there. You can never know what the outcome will be until you do it!

18

The Unexpected

Learning to expect the unexpected guards against complacency.

I HAD COMPANY at the 2007 Wildflower Triathlon held in San Antonio, California, on May 4. *Real Sports* with Bryant Gumble was planning to film me, and this was to be their first of many segments. The Wildflower race is well named, not only because of the abundance of yellow wildflowers dotting the countryside, but also because it can be a wild race. The area is out in no-man's-land on the reserve of Lake San Antonio where the swim takes place. The bike course is so riddled with hills that the worst of them has a mechanical Energizer bunny at the top to encourage the cyclists to keep climbing.

This race was to be the debut for my new Cannondale bike given me for the Spirit of Determination Award in the Hawaiian Ironman the previous October, and I was still getting used to it. I struggled up the top of the first of many hills without having to dismount, even though quite a few younger triathletes did.

At around mile 11, I was in the process of cycling past a woman on the right, which is where you are supposed to pass. But this was a huge race, and there are a lot of inexperienced people in it. Another woman pedaled up on my left and started chit-chatting, which made me very nervous, as you are not supposed to ride side by side unless in the process of passing, which must be completed in 15 seconds.

I was just about to introduce her to the fact that this could be considered drafting, when all of a sudden this guy shot between the two of us on my left, which was a no-no also. He cut too short in front of me, causing my front wheel to kiss his rear tire. I thought, "Oh, God, this is going to be a major pileup if I don't do something, but what can I do? If I go to my right, I'll bring down the woman I am trying to pass. If I turn to my left, there goes the chit-chatter."

I was sandwiched. "Please, God, let me bring my wheel over slightly to the right momentarily." I was hoping the man in question would have felt his rear wheel wobble when it touched my front wheel so he would pick up the pace. When I brought my wheel back into alignment, he had not advanced sufficiently. The contact unsettled him slightly, but I was the one to go down.

When this happened, all three involved stopped to help me out of the way of oncoming cyclists. Hobbling over to the side of the road, I felt a lot of pain in my left elbow. I tried to remount the bike, but when I got astride and leaned on the arrowbars I knew I wouldn't have enough strength in my injured arm to get me through the rest of this hilly course.

An ambulance was called. When it arrived it had already made another stop. I recognized its other passenger. She had asked me for a blessing before the race. When I got in the ambulance, I joked, "Isn't this a heck of a way to meet up with each other again?" She had been lying limp with eyes closed, hooked up to a breathing apparatus, but when she heard my voice her eyes popped open and she gave me a faint smile. I kept the conversation rolling to help her remain conscious.

It was a forty-five-minute ride to the nearest hospital in King City. So as not to interfere with the race, the ambulance drove over rough back roads, and the jolting only added to the pain. At the hospital, there was a considerable wait. I began shaking, I suppose from aftershock. Plus, I was still wearing a damp swim suit beneath my cycling clothes. Finally they threw a blanket over me and gave me a pair of terrycloth slippers so I could remove my cleated cycling shoes. All I needed was another fall on their slippery tile floors.

After some confusion and a second set of X-rays, I learned that I had three fractures in my left elbow, one in the ulna, one in the radius, and another elsewhere. The doctor put my arm in a half cast, wrapped it in an ACE bandage, gave me a sling and a prescription for pain medicine, then dismissed me with advice to see my own doctor after I returned home, which was four days hence. I had nothing with me—no money, no ID, no medical card, no way to get back to the race site where I had left my backpack. All my belongings were back there in the tent where I had shivered through the night. Just then, Bill Evans, the photographer employed by HBO to do the filming, called, saying, "I don't want to be invasive, but could I come to the hospital to see you?"

"Not only is it okay," I told him, "I would love for you to come and get me out of here. Will you please bring my backpack? It has all my credentials!" He did, and papers being filed, I was now free to leave. I hadn't had anything to eat since before the race. It was now 3:30 p.m. and unfortunately the hospital cafeteria had just closed. When we rolled into King City, Bill and his young assistant found a Subway and a Starbucks, where they graciously refueled me. They also talked the race personnel at Wildflower into finding someplace other than a tent for me to spend the night.

My friend Fred Goss and I drove back to Oakland the following day. He and his wife tried to persuade me to lay over with them a little longer, but I really needed to see my own doctor. Plus my friend in Portland, with whom I had left my car, was expecting me the following day. The Gosses pressured me no longer and waited with me to board the Amtrak at ten o'clock that evening. It was to be a seventeen-hour train ride from Oakland to Portland, with multiple stops along the way. Although Amtrak never stops very long, they are known for not being on schedule. Needless to say, I spent a very wakeful night.

At 6:30 the next morning the conductor announced we would have a fifteen-minute layover at Klamath Falls. I decided I needed some fresh air and wanted to use the station's restroom which would be a little roomier than the train's. I was careful to check my watch. When I came out of the restroom, I was shocked to see the train moving away. It had stopped only ten minutes. I noticed the conductor hanging out of the window of one of the cars and began yelling while running along after the train over very uneven rocky ground with arm in sling. He gave no indication that he even saw me.

As the train began to pick up speed, I was losing ground. Fearing that I would never make it, I prayed, "Lord, this is going to take another miracle. I need it now." Everything I carried with me to the race, plus the Advil, was on that train. I looked back at the depot to see how far I had gone. To my amazement, I saw a flock of people gathered outside waving me on, so I turned to resume running over the pebbly terrain. In so doing I saw the conductor was still hanging out of the window and noticed two red lights blinking farther down the tracks, one on either side.

Was it possible? Was this train truly slowing down? Now I was actually even with the car where the conductor was. But it was at least a two-foot stretch upward to the platform. How was I going to perform this feat? Thank God for long legs. The door handle was on my left, the same side as my damaged arm. I pulled myself up by crossing over with my right arm to grab the handle, swung one leg up while the other still dangled. When I planted myself on the threshold, the conductor bent down and pulled me up the rest of the way by the waist. Dealing with the mixed emotions of anger, relief, gratitude, and exhaustion, I'm not sure I even thanked him.

Now I had to find my way back to the car I'd been riding in, a ticklish task as the train began to pick up speed, weaving back and forth. I didn't want to risk being slammed against the walls. When I passed through one of the cars, someone who had seen the drama called out, "You are so lucky. Amtrak never stops for anyone." I snapped back, "They should have. They left five minutes ahead of time." But deep down in my heart I was spilling over with gratitude that God had again taken pity on his adventurous child.

That was not the end of the saga, however. My friend Barbara Larrain, with whom I had left my car, met me at the depot in Portland, but the train arrived too late for me to barrel back to Spokane for the seven-hour drive. Furthermore Barbara and

her husband were not about to let me go it alone with my injured arm. They coerced me into spending the night after calling
Spokane for a doctor's appointment the next morning. Barbara
insisted on coming along to do the driving even though she was
unaccustomed to a stick shift. We had scarcely gone less than
50 miles when the car exhibited problems.

A sheriff stopped to assist and lifted the hood to see what
was wrong. Smoke came pouring out, which he diagnosed as a
burned-out clutch, and called the AAA driver he knew in the
nearest town 6 miles away. The tow truck driver even went out
of his way to get us to the closest town some 48 miles away by
skillfully combining both our AAA cards in such a way that we
would be charged nothing extra. At the garage the repairman announced immediately that the car had a transmission problem. I
told him I'd feel better if he put the car on a hoist to examine it
first, as I had been told the problem was with the clutch.

While waiting for this repair, Barbara and I walked around
looking for some place to hydrate and get nourishment. It was
now 4 p.m. and a sweltering 100 degrees. We'd had nothing to
eat since breakfast, and the shop didn't even have water available. We found ourselves at a used car lot only a few blocks
away. One of the men who worked there overheard us say we'd
have to spend the night somewhere in this town. He thought-
fully suggested he call his wife to see if we could stay with them.
Then he lent us a Suburu to get to their house some 12 miles
away. We were taken care of until the clutch was replaced and
we could get on the road the following day. The angelic assistance of sheriff, tow truck driver, and salesman did not go unac-
knowledged. However it did occur to me that my trusty old 1995

Ford Escort wagon might be falling apart at the same rate as my maturing body!

When we rolled into Spokane, my doctor was waiting, even though we were a half an hour late. "Well, it looks as if your arm has remained settled in the half cast no matter what you have been through—chasing a train, being towed, sleeping in strange places. However, you have only a fifty-fifty chance that the arm will heal in place without needing surgery." He offered to put on another cast, but I was adamant. "Oh, no, please don't bother."

I had a secret reason. With just the bandage wound around the top part, I could slip these magnets into the sleeve, which would possibly promote healing. I also dosed up on extra calcium. By removing the bandage and sitting out in the sun, even though it was over ninety degrees, I got some natural vitamin D. Furthermore I walked everywhere I needed to go, even if it was six miles, to enhance my circulation. The doctor wanted to see me the following week since he thought there was a good chance I would need surgery. "No matter what," he said, "it will take at least ten weeks to heal." Usually I take six weeks to heal from a broken bone. Since there were several fractures involved, plus my maturing years, he gave me a bit more time.

I murmured to myself, "No, it's not going to take ten weeks. He'll be surprised." With God's help, I knew I had to cut that time in half in order to participate in the National Amateur Championship triathlon the next month to procure a spot on Team USA for the ITU World Championship. This race was the one and only qualifier.

Five weeks later, the doctor ordered some new X-rays. After reviewing them he pronounced in amazement, "Well you can resume speed if you haven't already." Unbeknownst to him, I had already done some water jogging and had been regularly walking long distances to get where I needed to go, since I could neither drive my stick shift nor ride my bike to get around.

Given the official go-ahead, I was relieved, and rushed home to get on my bike but was suddenly filled with trepidation. I was not prepared for this reaction! What had the accident done to my psyche? I had concentrated so hard on pouring all my energy into healing I never thought beyond that. When I finally got the okay to train again, I had no energy left for motivation. This, coupled with a new fear about remounting my bike, left me overwhelmed. "Lord, what is going on?" I have had accidents galore but had never had a reaction like this. Back in 1984 when I broke my hip, I had been scared, but the darkness of spirit that was besetting me now was something entirely new.

After mulling it over, it occurred to me that this accident was the very first in my twenty-eight years of competing that had actually happened within the thick of the competition itself. In my Hawaiian 2000 accident, I'd been trashed by the elements, not by a fellow cyclist. Now I was about to face competition again in just one week at the National Amateur Championships, having had no chance to train for the past six weeks and left with emotional scars.

As I stood there holding my bikè in trepidation, I heard that familiar inner voice: "If you don't get on that bike *now*, you probably never will again." This thought overrode my fears. It was all I could do to force my leg over the bar, get clipped into my pedals, and go out on a short bike ride. I set a goal of just five miles. Once I got going, however, everything fell into place, and

I actually put in about fifteen miles, coming back with my confidence restored.

The following week I set out for the 340-mile drive to Hagg Lake, but my troubles weren't over yet. As I was driving through an intersection, a big van pulled smack in front of me from the left even though I had the green light to go straight. I had nowhere to turn without going up on the curb. The right side of his rear bumper caught the left side of my front bumper, denting it, breaking the headlight, and leaving some cracks on the fender. Thank heaven for another triathlete who was coming from the opposite direction and witnessed the accident. Otherwise, I am not sure the driver of the van would have stopped.

This encounter caused me to flash back to my bike accident and rattled my nerves all over again. My confidence level was now undermined for the next day's race. Plus on race day it was chilly and overcast. After the swim portion of the race, I was shaking so badly I could scarcely get out of my wet suit and mount the bike. Then there was an immediate uphill climb to get to the bike course. The younger hotshots came shooting by, edging me over to the side of the road. To continue safely, I had to ride on the bumpy shoulder, jarring my newly unprotected arm. It was purely the grace of God that I managed to push through it all to capture the gold and a berth on Team USA for the eighteenth consecutive year.

That was in June, only six weeks after my injured elbow at Wildflower. Just a week later was the Ford Half Ironman 70.3 triathlon at Lake Stevens, Washington. Even though it was twice the distance, the Lake Stevens race had a totally different atmosphere. Here the athletes were relaxed, friendly, and considerate of one another.

A month later, in July, I went on to Colorado for the Boulder Peak Triathlon, a new event for me with a hill that goes straight up for a mile. The high spirits and camaraderie helped me through it. Two nights before the race I was asked to speak at a fund-raiser banquet where the triathletes were an enthusiastic and receptive bunch.

In August I did the Long Bridge Swim across Lake Pend Oreille, from Sand Point, Idaho, to the opposite side, a strange distance of 1.76 miles. The next day I offered to run 13.1 miles in the Troika Half Ironman as a team member for a gal who had a leg injury and couldn't do the whole triathlon herself. She did the swim and bike, and I ran the 13.1 miles for her. Five days later I drove to Boise to do Emmett's Most Excellent Triathlon for the first time and gave out the awards at the children's race the day before. Next on the docket was the Canadian Ironman slated for the last Sunday in August.

Despite my injury, I finished the 2007 Canadian Ironman in 16:40:29, which bettered my time of 2005 when I first opened the 75 to 79 age group for women. This was a welcome turn of events, because the year before I had had to abort the race eight miles from the finish line. I was running alone in the dark and advised I probably wouldn't reach the finish until after one o'clock in the morning. I was told that the police were worried about me being out there alone in the dark, so I accepted a ride back and called it quits, which was a first in my seventeen years of doing the Canadian Ironman not to finish what I had started. In the end I was relieved that this year had worked out as well as it did.

19

Fast Forward and Rewind

If life didn't have challenges,
it wouldn't be worth living.

THROUGHOUT THE SPRING and summer of 2007 I had squeezed in sixteen events altogether. In the midst of it all, I had a birthday coming up on July 24. It struck me that I was turning seventy-seven in the seventh month of 2007. How often, if ever, does this happen in one's lifetime? It seemed cause for some sort of celebration.

But what? How? Throw a party for myself? No! However, I decided if I didn't, no one else would, so I turned the occasion into a fund-raiser for my parish, which had been going through some hard times. We could have a wine-tasting party, coupled with a silent auction in the Knights of Columbus hall. It would be open to parishioners and personal friends. All they would be asked to do was to bring some item for the auction or the wine-tasting table.

During Mass one day, this distracting thought caught me: "What a risk you are taking! How do you know how many people will even respond?" Then came the realization: "You are stepping out in faith for a cause bigger than yourself. Go for it." Had I not listened to the small voice which said, "I will provide," I could not have done it. Nor could I have pulled it off without the cooperation and enthusiastic suggestions of our parish secretary. When I asked how many she thought we should plan for, she said without hesitation, "Oh, seventy-five to a hundred."

Still I was a little concerned about how it would all work out, so devised a backup plan. I arranged to have a Bible and a couple of index cards on a table by the entrance. One card would say, "If there isn't enough wine, read John 2:1–11," the Marriage Feast at Cana where Jesus performed his first miracle of turning water into wine. The other card could say, "If there isn't enough food, refer to Matthew 15:32–38 and Mark 8:1–10" (Jesus miraculously multiplies the loaves and fishes to feed the crowd). That was my backup!

As it happened, there were exactly the number of people present that the secretary had predicted with more than enough food and wine and an abundance of items for the auction. Everyone, including the Bishop and Parish Priest, enjoyed mixing with the sundry guests.

I have always had the initial faith that if God put something on my mind and in my heart, it could and should be done, but both elements must work together—mind to initiate it and the heart to propel it. Otherwise, it is likely to be a lost cause or a frivolous undertaking, instead of an adventure in Faith. Over the years, I have been involved in both, but my drive has always been to answer the call and let God do the rest.

*   *   *

Three days after my seventy-seventh birthday, I discovered that seven might not be such a lucky number after all. While I was slicing an avocado for my birthday dinner at a friend's house, the knife slipped, creating a deep groove across three fingers of my left hand, necessitating a trip to the ER. Being a Friday the place was packed before I got there at 7 p.m. I feared I might lose all my blood waiting for three hours to be seen. By midnight the one and only nurse stitched me up temporarily and advised me to go see a doctor on Monday because I might have sliced a ligament on my middle finger. On Sunday my hand inadvertently slipped off the tub while I was bathing, so I removed the soggy bandage and found I could slightly bend my middle finger. Consequently, I skipped the doctor's appointment, keeping my Monday appointment at jail instead. I wore protective binding during the 2007 Canadian Ironman a month later. Finishing in 16:40:29 gained me another Age Group first place.

Two weeks later, now September, I competed in the Ultra-Max Triathlon, a Half Ironman distance at the Innsbruck Resort about an hour's drive west of Saint Louis. The race director, Mark Livesey, always asked me to say a prayer at the shoreline before the event. As we gathered, I learned that earlier in the year there had been a death in this lake during one of his other events. In my prayer, I suggested we all offer the race in memory of our deceased fellow triathlete.

When I was running out of the swim up toward the bike transition, I was accidentally knocked down when some man shoved past me. Then, still barefoot, I ran over an embedded peg that was cordoning off the transition area. My big toe got the worst of it. Nevertheless, I got through the bike portion. But on the run coming down a hilly section, my toe began throbbing badly. Until then, I had forgotten about running over the peg and thought my foot was probably stressed from being in cycling shoes too long or running over uneven terrain.

The next week, while still in Saint Louis attending an event for one of my Alma Maters, I had to wear dress shoes and could hardly squeeze my left foot into the shoe. The swelling had not subsided, and I knew something was wrong. By the time I got back to Spokane, I figured I probably had a fracture; but since the Hawaiian Ironman was coming up in just four weeks, I decided to wait it out rather than seek a doctor.

Once in Hawaii, I was too busy with the HBO photographers on their third assignment to catch me in action during the Ironman to be mindful of my toe. I got through the swim, but about sixty miles into the bike portion my foot, as well as my stomach, began to bother me. The weather was also beginning to heat up, so I actually got off my bike to take in some fluids. It was then I realized that I was beginning to feel nauseated well before the run. When I remounted the bike, I consciously shifted my position on the pedals to relieve my aching foot, saying to the Lord, "You know I envy those who don't have to do the run today."

Earlier, just five miles into the race, my chain had come off and I had had to walk my bike up the hill, where I could remount. Now I dismounted once more just to touch terra firma and sniff the air. The HBO people were shouting something across the way, trying to urge me on. I think they knew something I didn't, that time was running out for the bike cutoff. When I got back on my bike I wasn't worried about time, as I had never had trouble finishing the bike cutoff before. Close to town, a noncompetitor came alongside me on the bike course saying, "Come on, Sister, get in front of me. You gotta go!"

I thought I had been doing okay, pushing it for all I was worth; but when I got to the bike transition, I was told, "I am sorry, Sister, you missed the bike cutoff by thirty seconds. You can't go on the run." The cameramen were there; but it wasn't the moment they were expecting to capture. Rather than being distraught, I was actually relieved. Glancing up to heaven, I declared, "Father knows best." Left to myself, I probably would have gone out on the run and done myself in, perhaps further delaying the healing of my foot.

Two other women behind me just missed the cutoff too, and one was falling apart emotionally. I gave them each a hug, trying to console them with, "It's okay. Look what we are being spared." As for myself, I knew my foot had had enough stress with the 112 miles of cycling. I might not have made the run cutoff by midnight anyway.

Nonetheless in retrospect, I reflected on the thirty seconds or more lost in the bike transition after the swim. I was stunned to see one of the announcers there with the media behind him, smiling at me as he kept a firm grip on my bicycle while the cameras were rolling. Nobody is supposed to be in the transition area except the triathletes. I think it took me at least a minute to wrench my bike loose from him. But for that loss of time, I probably could have made the cutoff. However, it was not meant to be. I had at least done two-thirds of the 2007 Hawaiian Ironman.

I still had two more trips ahead of me before the 2007 triathlon season was over. In Clearwater, Florida, I engaged in the inaugural 70.3 Ford Ironman World Championship on November 10, covering a Half Ironman distance of 70.3 miles. I just sailed through it and had wonderful company. No one can tell me that a full Ironman is just twice a Half Ironman. It is much more!

The woman who had gotten the Determination Award the year I did at the Hawaiian Ironman, Sarah Reinertsen, was also there at Clearwater. She is a one-legged amputee and had been unable to finish the Hawaiian Ironman in 2004, but came back as a finisher in 2005 to receive the same award I had received in 2006, a new Cannondale. Rudy Garcia-Tolson, a double amputee, was also here and finished shortly after I did. Then there was eighty-one-year-old Robert McKeague. He had opened the 80-plus Age Group for men in the 2005 Hawaiian Ironman. As the media surrounded us, you would have thought the whole thing had been staged. There we were—the two male and female amputees and the two oldest male and female finishers all together, still congratulating each other in the chute when we found ourselves surrounded by the media, cameras flashing away.

That year *Runner's World* magazine selected me as one of the candidates for their 2007 Heroes Award for my performance in the 2006 Hawaiian Ironman. I couldn't help but look back on my journey. When I started out and set my sights on the 1982 Boston marathon, women forty and over had to run a sub-3:30 marathon. I was twelve years beyond this when I had qualified at age fifty-two with a mere forty-eight seconds to spare. Now, twenty-four years later, being the last official finisher of the 2006 Hawaii Ironman championship, and being recognized for that, seemed to me a bit ironic. But! Perhaps 2007 was a lucky year for me after all! Despite all the injuries and disappointments, there was something at the end of the rainbow. The trophy awarded me was a ten-pound pot of gold, the gilded foot of Winged Mercury.

20

Going the Distance

*It is how we handle our challenges
that makes us who and what we are.*

AFTER I RECEIVED the *Runner's World* Heroes Award, another recipient, Dave McGilliviray, the race director of the Boston Marathon, came up to me and said, "Sister, any time you'd like to do the Boston Marathon again, you're in." I thanked him but said the only marathons I did anymore were those connected to an Ironman triathlon and that lately, because of my stomach issues, those marathons involved hardly any running, mostly walking.

I still had not found the right combination of nourishment that worked for me over these long distances. For seventeen years, I had been something of a camel, getting along with a lot less water than other people. I couldn't count on that any more: Now I have to try to take in a lot of little sips more frequently, since I can't manage big gulps. I am still learning that as you get older, your system changes, and frankly, I don't know what to do about it.

But before long, the thought of doing the Boston Marathon again teased me. I realized that in April I was going to be on the East Coast anyway for the World Harmony Run in New York City, a global relay that had been organized by the guru, athlete, author, and East Indian philosopher, Sri Chinmoy, to spread peace among nations. I had been invited to help carry the torch for the opening of that event. Though Sri Chinmoy didn't live to meet me—he had died while I was in Hawaii doing the Ironman in October—the World Harmony Run was still launched as planned.

The Boston Marathon was scheduled just two weeks later. I also realized that the Saint Anthony's Triathlon in Florida, my first triathlon of 2008, was only six days after the Boston race, so why not take in all three events? It made financial sense to just stay on the East Coast instead of flying back and forth across the country. So, in November, I made the decision to set my sights on doing the Boston Marathon once again. It would be exactly twenty-five years after I had done my first one. Furthermore, it would be an interesting experiment to find out if I could actually run a marathon by itself without putting in a 2.4-mile swim and a 112-mile bike race in front of it. Maybe I'd even avoid getting nauseous.

Of course, winter was coming in Spokane, and it turned out to be even worse than usual. It was one of the most severe and prolonged we have ever had, and the roads were not clear enough to run on until the end of February. By March, with the race just six weeks away, I succeeded in working in only three ten-mile runs on no build up and had been on my bike just five times when I encountered a major setback.

The sixth time out on the bike, I was headed to the library and barreling through an intersection when a car, due to a change of lights, turned right in front of me. To avoid a head-on collision, I swerved, but spun out on some loose gravel that still remained on the road from the snow. Instantaneously, I knew I was going down and shifted my weight so as to land on my right hip in order to preserve the "scrap metal" in my left hip, a souvenir from my 1984 hit-and-run accident resulting in a broken hip. By this maneuver I escaped injury, so I thought, although my bike tights did not. Some pedestrians helped get me and my bicycle out of the road. The only problem was that I was still clipped into my pedals when they tried to get the bike off me.

Since I had no time to go home from the library to change, I went directly to Mass, ripped tights and all. By the time I got home, I realized I was really hurting. Apparently the pedestrians, in their eagerness to pull me off the bike to avoid oncoming traffic, had yanked too hard with me still clipped in. In past accidents, I had broken bones to contend with, but I had never felt anything like this before. I suspected it was a pulled groin muscle. If so, there was no use going to the doctor. I figured it was just a matter of time—but how much time?

The Boston Marathon was scarcely a month and a half away. Up to this point, I had only been able to put in thirty miles of running. Now I couldn't run at all! The best I could do was a painful, awkward shuffle. I wondered if I should cancel. Then I thought, "Well, I am going to be in the East anyway, and there is no rule about how long it can take to shuffle through a marathon. Perhaps if I alternate running a mile, race-walking a mile, and walking a mile, I can get through it."

I practiced doing this. My time was practically the same, no matter which mode I chose. I did my multiplication tables and realized this was not going to be fast enough to meet the requalification time for women seventy-plus, which had to be five hours and fifteen minutes or less. But this did not mean they would pull me off the course, so I decided to go for it regardless of my compromised condition.

When I left home on April 9 for the first of the East Coast events, the World Harmony Run, I had to face the fact that I had absolutely no adequate training mileage behind me for the prestigious Boston Marathon that followed. I heal quickly, but this injury was taking longer than recovering from broken bones. Although time was not on my side, I trusted that God was.

The World Harmony Runners gathered in Battery Park at the foot of Manhattan. It was a glorious spring day as we were ferried over to the Statue of Liberty for the start. When we disembarked, famed athlete Carl Lewis was handed the lighted torch and ran it up to the statue, where a small group was waiting at the foot for the brief ceremony. We returned to Battery Park, where the other runners organized to take turns running the five miles up to Dag Hammarskjöld Plaza near the United Nations for the official ceremony.

I was a little concerned because at the same time the torch for the Olympics in Beijing was being demonstrated against in San Francisco. I thought, "Uh-oh, here we are, running through the streets of New York City carrying this flaming torch. How are people going to react?" As I was running along with the torch, only one person on the street yelled, "What's that for?" I yelled back, "We're running for peace and harmony."

"Oh, okay."

At the UN, representatives from some seventy nations were present, carrying torches and flags. Similar World Harmony relay runs were taking place on the continents of Africa, Europe, Asia, and Australia.

Standing there, I realized I had just run five miles without any complaint. I had not run this distance since the bike spill on March 2. Maybe there was hope for the Boston Marathon after all. It was now just eleven days away. That close to a marathon, most people are easing off any kind of training. But here I was, doing just the opposite, trying to step up my meager mileage.

At the ceremony near the UN, Lewis led the group in a moment of silence for world peace. The World Harmony Run officials asked five of us—Carl Lewis, Billie Jean King, Russell Simmons, Roberta Flack, and me—to come to the stage. They honored us with a beautiful medal hung on a yellow and royal blue ribbon.

It was not until the next day that I turned the medal over to find a quote from the late guru Sri Chinmoy engraved on the reverse side: "To change the world around you, give to the world what you have and serve the world with what you are." This thought really grabbed me. After all, isn't that what life is all about?

Before I left, I asked the woman who had brought me to Sri Chinmoy's attention and with whom I had stayed what Sri Chinmoy's favorite colors had been. I don't even know what made me ask that question. Without hesitation she replied, "Yellow and blue." I gulped. These were the very colors I had chosen to make up my wardrobe before this three-week sojourn to the East Coast.

After this World Harmony event, on April 12, I went upstate to Cambridge, New York, to be with my friend Mary Muncil while waiting it out for the Boston Marathon. I tried to work in a little training. I had two opportunities for a long run. Since I had no car, I couldn't measure the mileage exactly, but sensed I was probably running about a half marathon, or 13.1 miles each time. On Monday, seven days before the Boston Marathon, and then again on Wednesday, five days before the race, I ran this same distance. Later I asked my friend to measure the distance in her car. It was precisely what I had sensed it to be. I was elated, but at the same time realistic: After all, this distance was just half required of the marathon.

So far, my training for Boston had consisted solely of three 10-mile runs before my accident, one 5-mile run with the World Harmony runners, and now two 13.1-mile runs the week before—a total of 61 miles within two months, hardly what you would call training for a marathon. Would this be enough to carry me? "Lord, I've done the best I could. The rest is up to you."

After Mary and I arrived in Boston, I needed to calculate what time I expected to complete the marathon, so that she could be there to meet me at the finish. I knew that women over seventy had to finish the race in less than five hours fifteen minutes in order to requalify. At best, I figured I'd be lucky to toe the finish in five and one-half hours, or more likely, six, if nothing went wrong.

It was foggy and the temperature was only forty-five degrees when they bused us to the starting point in Framingham. I was amazed at the crowd. There were more than twenty-four thousand runners, where twenty-five years ago there had been roughly six thousand people. Back then, it had taken six minutes after the gun went off just to get to the starting line. Now everything had become more advanced through technology so that all runners wore ankle chips in order to record their exact times.

I lined up with the runners in my designated group. Ours was the last section to start. Once I began running, I felt as if I were being gently nudged forward from the rear by two kindly spirits, those of Sri Chinmoy and Jesus. As the race progressed, I did not even feel as if I were exerting myself. My nourishment was minimal—in all, four Clif Bar Sureshot Gels, a packet of Enlyten strips, water, and a bottle of Fusion, which I had sampled at the Expo two days earlier and seemed to set well with my digestive system. Other than that, there was nothing I seemed to need.

The entire twenty-six miles was still lined with cheering spectators even though we were the last contingent. When we reached Wellesley College, just short of the halfway mark, the enthusiasm of those Wellesley girls was absolutely amazing. They certainly knew how to pump up our spirits. It was infectious and fed us with sustained energy. When I ran the few hills before Heartbreak Hill, I thought they weren't much. When I got to Heartbreak Hill itself, I didn't know I was on it until I overheard someone talking. However, during the last two miles of the marathon, I could feel my legs tightening. That was when I had to push. Until that point, I felt like I had more or less been gliding.

When I ran across the finish line and then saw my time, I could not believe it. It said, not six hours, not five hours, but 4:42:41. It was truly amazing. I had done my first Boston at the age of fifty-two. Now I had done it again at seventy-eight. Of course it took me an hour longer, but I was in awe that I'd done it that quickly under the circumstances—way beyond my wildest estimations!

I was still in the finishing chute looking for Mary when my friend Allen Cherkasky came up all sweaty and huffing behind me. "Sister, you did it again. You got in front of me. Weren't those hills awful?"

"Umm-uh. What hills?" I countered. This remark nearly killed him. He was in his forties. His wife, who had done the race, was in bed at the hotel, and one of his sons who had finished was also laid out in the room. All were worn to a frazzle by the time Mary and I met up with them at their hotel.

By the time Mary and I found our way to the awards ceremony, they had already awarded my age group. But I learned that at seventy-eight, I had been the oldest female to finish, and also had come in third in the seventy-plus women's age group. A month later, I received a beautiful heavy lead crystal bowl with fluted edging and the Boston Marathon insignia etched on it. Since I hadn't been present to accept it they'd shipped it to me. It was fortunate for me that I had been late for the awards ceremony. There was no way I could have hauled this three-pound lead crystal bowl around for the remainder of my journey. I like to think it was not only God's sense of timing, but His sense of humor that preserved me from becoming a beast of burden. And guess what? The finishing medal I received had the same blue and yellow ribbon as the World Harmony Run medal, Sri Chinmoy's favorite colors.

A week later the same colors popped up at the Saint Anthony's Triathlon in Saint Petersburg, Florida. A blessed presence seemed to have surrounded me since the World Harmony Run. Even though I had never met Sri Chinmoy as planned, he was definitely making me aware of his influence.

21

Encountering the Unforeseen

I never look at anything as defeat,
but consider all adversities as opportunities.

FOR THE FIRST spring event of 2009 in Florida, I came out of hibernation with even less training than usual. Spokane had broken the all-time record for snowfall during December, with the lowest temperature ever recorded for December 16 with a sub 17 degrees. I was ready for some sunshine. But even in Florida the weather was iffy. For two days before the Saint Anthony's race in Saint Petersburg, the wind was so strong the water was belching whitecaps. In fact, the winds had churned the water so badly that the race director decided to cancel the swim for the Age Groupers on race day. Even some of the Pros, who were permitted to go for the swim, had great difficulty.

The bike portion went well enough for me despite the wind, but I had gone only three miles on the run, when all of a sudden my right leg seized up so badly I could hardly move. None the less I shuffled the last three miles to the finish. There at the finish, a chiropractor, whom I knew, offered to work on my leg. The swelling was still evident however, and he recommended I continue to ice it. I iced the leg for several days before taking off for the long flight to Saint Croix in the Virgin Islands for the Beat the Beast 70.3 triathlon. There was no way to relieve my leg on the plane by elevating or icing. I was headed for the fourth time to one of the most notably challenging Half Ironman distance races, nicknamed after that famous hill known as the Beast.

During the swim, I actually forgot about my leg. But there was another annoying factor. This one woman kept gnawing at my feet and clawing at my arms for the entire 1.2 miles. In utter frustration, I reached out sideways with my bad leg to push her away. That did my leg no good. When I got out of the water just in front of her, she ran by me, saying, "I hope you didn't mind my keeping up with you." My emphatic response was, "I have never had such a leech in my life!" Her rejoinder: "I couldn't help it. I needed to." It made me realize she desperately wanted to qualify for the Hawaiian Ironman slot available and was using me to assist her in the swim.

The run was challenging enough, especially the portion around the perimeter of the Buccaneer golf course. In the meantime, ABC television had spotted me and begun following me on the run. I was doing okay until mile 9, when all of a sudden my leg seized up again. I had four miles left to go in this handicapped condition. Even though I knew I would somehow finish, it would not be in enough time to earn the coveted Hawaiian Ironman slot for my age group. My one thought was simply to get it over with. Although disappointed, I was pleased to have finished as the oldest person ever to have attempted this race.

I also knew I had one more chance to qualify for the Hawaiian Ironman at the Canadian Ironman scheduled for the end of August.

After I got home, my leg was still not down to normal size. I was advised to get a special test to make sure there was no clotting. "If there is, and you continue on, you could be a goner," said the physical therapist. Fortunately, no clotting was discovered, and my leg healed on its own over a course of five weeks with no one knowing quite what went wrong. I've never been old before, so this was all new to me!

On the Fourth of July, I did the five-mile Firecracker Run in Spokane having not trained for a month and got through it fine. That same weekend I went on a thirty-five-mile bike ride when the heat had climbed to ninety-three degrees, so I was pretty wasted after that weekend, but two triathlons were coming up soon, so this was training for those—the San Francisco Triathlon on July 12, followed by the Vineman Half Ironman in Santa Rosa, California, a week later on July 18.

As it turned out, each event in 2009 brought its own snafus. In the San Francisco Triathlon, there was confusion. We had to count our own laps, amounting to twelve, on the bike course. Well, I went one too many, which of course affected my time. At the Vineman a week later, I arrived too late for the orientation and had no idea about the location of the markers for the swim course in the Russian River. As I was swimming my way through, I saw two buoys close together and mistook those as markers for the turnaround. I had just established a good rhythm when I saw all these blue caps swimming past and realized my mistake. This was the group that had started in front of mine, so I swam back to the middle until I saw a boat with a race marshal and asked where the turnaround was. It was further ahead. So I wound up swimming a little over the allotted distance.

I lectured myself afterward: "Well, you put in an extra lap on the bike in San Francisco, and now you have put in some extra mileage on the swim here at the Vineman. You are showing your age, Cookie." As it turned out I was the oldest competitor in both events, with no men in my age group at all, so it was easier to excuse my *faux pas*.

On the run portion in the Vineman, I rediscovered the virtue of running in my head instead of concentrating on my body. When I started out on the run, I began reminiscing about the first Vineman I had done back in 2001, after I had turned seventy-one. The race director had given me the gift of free entry and a ride in a hot air balloon. Now, as I was running along, I was recalling the sensation of that balloon ride, which was so different from anything I had ever experienced. It was so much fun soaring above the ground and hearing the birds singing below, listening to the dogs bark, and spotting deer on the move. I began amusing myself by composing a haiku about the experience as I ran:

Gliding above birds
Earth's inhabitants below
Hot air balloon drifts.

I kept repeating that in my head for a while, committing it to memory. That's when I was aware of running well. My mind was so busy it put my body on cruise control so I discovered getting zoned out can be a good thing while running at least.

*   *   *

The year 2009 had been a strange one from the start. I had but four races left now. Rolling in to the bike-run transition of the Lake Stevens Half Ironman in Washington State on August 16, I had another fluky experience. Of the six recent events thus far, only one had gone smoothly. At Lake Stevens, a portion of us on the bike segment were misdirected, so we missed doing the second lap on the bike. I told the official in charge what had happened and said I wanted to get back on course, but she responded, "Never mind, just give me your race number, bring the bike in, and go out on the run. Your time will be adjusted." She missed the point! I really wanted to do the entire fifty-six miles on the bike as training for the Canadian Ironman, which was coming up two weeks later. I was disappointed, and diddled around in transition, trying to decide whether or not to go out on the run.

At the awards ceremony, they didn't call out any sixty-plus or seventy-plus categories for women, which seemed strange because there had been some competitors in both age groups, including myself. When I asked the announcer why seventy-plus hadn't been mentioned, he said, "You were disqualified for not finishing the course." I said, "What? I was told that because I was misdirected, the time would be adjusted." Guess it was too much math for them since it affected twenty or thirty people! Nonetheless, some of them were hoping to use this race as a qualifier for the 70.3 championships in Clearwater, Florida.

That over, I was now engaged in the Canadian Ironman 2009, held in Penticton, British Columbia, on August 30. I was grateful just to have finished. Weather-wise, it was one of the best years I could remember. The water temperature with wet suits was very pleasant and doable. The air temperature was neither too hot nor too cold. I had a good swim with a fairly fast transition, but I was pushing it on the run because this was the first time they had instituted a cutoff time for the halfway mark on the run course. I knew I would really have to keep my legs churning for those first 13.1 miles.

Even while on the bike I could sense my stomach was not going to be very cooperative on the run. By the time I had run to the 13.1-mile marker, night had fallen, making for poor visibility. Now I was reduced to walking, conscious I was not doing so in a straight line, due in part to darkness and to fatigue resulting from not taking in enough nourishment.

One of the participants behind me noticed my predicament. When he caught up to me, he said, "Just lean on me," placing his arm around my shoulder to steady me. We walked like this for a while until I straightened up a bit. Then he released his arm and reached for my hand just to keep me secured. He introduced himself as a member of the Canadian Navy stationed in Halifax. We kept pacing this way mile after mile for twelve more.

Since he was wearing a watch, he could calculate how many minutes it took for us to do each mile. I suggested, "Let's run downhill if we can, and walk the uphill." He was very patient in his prodding, yet both of us knew we were going against time. He could have finished the race a lot sooner if he hadn't been trying to bring me in. My urging him to go on was in vain. Obviously he was the sort of person who got more joy out of helping others than in thinking of himself. When we got within two and a half miles of the finish, I asked his name. He just said, "Terry."

"Terry, I think we really have to run from now on, no matter what happens." He agreed. As soon as I spotted the finish line, I bolted toward it, finishing in 16:54:30, breaking my previous 75–79 age group record by two minutes. Without my angel from Halifax, whose full name I learned later was Terry Moore, I'd probably still be out on the course.

At the awards ceremony, there was a standing ovation for this seventy-nine-year-old lady and for a seventy-eight-year-old male finisher, France Cokan. We were the only ones in our respective age groups. It was nice to have someone up on stage with me. When I am up there all by myself, I feel a bit lonely. Of course, my real hero was Terry Moore, the young man who so patiently guided me to the finish, the angel who made it possible for me to finish by midnight and thus qualify for the Hawaiian Ironman five weeks later.

I had never had such a hard time recovering as I did from this Canadian Ironman. Usually I get out and run or bike the next day after a major event of that sort. But four days after this one, I was still feeling it in my legs. I think having to walk as long as I did used different muscles than running. I had not trained for long-distance walking! It also occurred to me that as I advance in years I will probably require more angels. I will remain on the lookout. They may not know they are angels, but I surely do when they appear.

Next loomed the ITU World Championship on the Gold Coast in Australia, scheduled for September 12. Once there, I connected with some of the other women triathletes from Team USA, and we drove over the bike course. There had been talk that maybe we wouldn't be allowed to wear wet suits for the swim, so one of these gals and I tested the waters without them. It nearly took our breath away, and I was in for only seven minutes. I knew we'd be in four times as long for the actual swim on race day just two days hence. Many of us were really concerned about having to swim without wet suits, so I said to everyone, "You know there is power in prayer. The more, the better, so let's all pray that the powers-that-be make the right decision." Then I myself prayed, "Lord, no more fretting. I'm placing us in your hands."

The weather had been nice, but the day before the race it clouded up and got breezy, cooling the water enough so that we were allowed to wear wet suits. For each age division, they sent the women out first. Our group, being the oldest, was last among the women, but just in front of the younger male hotshots. Soon they caught up to us making waves as they slapped past us in the water, making us even more tentative as this was affecting our rhythm trying to dodge them.

But it was the bike segment that was really horrendous. The course itself was not difficult. In fact, it contained no hills or technical turns, which surprised me. What was awful was the congestion, especially on the second bike lap. The younger men came by in hordes, defying the drafting rules. They shot by in packs. Just when I thought I had gained a little breathing room and could stretch out on the arrow bars, I sensed another pack coming along, without even looking behind me.

I was just about to get on my arrow bars when I heard an Aussie behind me yell at another cyclist, "What are you *doing*, mate?" This alerted me to the approach of a pack, so I held steady, trying not to deviate a fraction of an inch. In the very next moment, a guy whipped by me on the left side, which was a no-no while the rest of the pack was passing me on the right. Had I faltered even a fraction of an inch, there would have been contact. If I had gone down, I probably would have brought the whole pack with me. From then on, I was totally attentive. It was with a sigh of relief that I brought the bike back into transition having seen carnage here and there along the route—bikes and bodies bent out of shape—the consequence of reckless riding in total disregard of the rules.

Once on the run, I was relieved that I was able to do the whole 6.2 miles without stopping. I was also grateful for having put in a good race, finishing in 3:15:58 and earning the gold for Team USA in the women's 75–79 division.

Later I learned that Kathy Felix, a U.S. team member in her mid-fifties, had been badly injured in one of the crashes and was hospitalized in Brisbane. Following the championship I wound up in Brisbane after doing some sightseeing along the Sunshine Coast with a friend who had joined me from Tasmania. The day before my departure I was able to visit with Kathy in the hospital. Her hip had been so torqued by the impact that it had gone through her pancreas and her leg had stuck out at a right angle. She had undergone surgery, first in the hospital on the Gold Coast where the race was held, and then had been brought to Brisbane, where she was fighting infection. Her color was not good, but her attitude was.

She had no recollection of the accident, which was a saving grace. I encouraged Kathy, "Your body is just being redesigned, and you are going to be in better shape than ever once you heal," and I prayed with her, blessing her on the forehead as I did so. After our visit, she already looked heaps better. Her last words to me as I left were, "In your travels, if you ever get near where

I live in California, please feel free to stay with my husband and myself. Our kids are out of the house now and I would love to have you." I thought, how gracious of her, so battered and in pain, yet still thinking of others. What a beautiful lesson in selflessness.

Triathlon and Ironman competitors are like that, with fellow sufferers looking out for one another.

It was a long trip home, longer than usual. The Sydney airport had been shut down because of a terrible dust storm. Flights were backed up. I missed two international flights to the West Coast of the USA and had two days of airport and airplane living. When I finally landed in Seattle, it was without my checked luggage, my bike. Having waited for it to appear in customs in the San Francisco airport for as long as I could before my connecting flight to Seattle, I had to just leave it all to God and dash to another concourse to pick up my return flight to Seattle. I could never have made that dash pushing a bike over unknown territory to yet another concourse. Again Father knew best. What is seemingly inconvenient at the time ends up being a saving grace.

Because my flight was delayed, it was nearly dark when I finally reached Seattle. I still had a six-hour drive back to Spokane, and I hadn't slept in two days. I was okay for an hour and a half of the drive, but when full darkness set in there was nothing for me to focus on ahead of me, and I began to succumb to drowsiness. I actually felt one of my hands slip from the wheel, which jerked me back to consciousness. Fortunately, there were no other cars on the road at the time for me to come into contact with.

I prayed, "Lord, just let me keep alert until I reach the next town." There I intended to stop for a milkshake or something to perk me up. By the time I got to Ritzville, sixty miles shy of Spokane, there was scarcely anything open. I did find a fast-food place that had just locked their doors, but they were willing to serve me through their drive-up window. When I got home, I literally fell into bed without even turning on the lights. I was even grateful I had no checked luggage to contend with.

My bike finally caught up with me in Spokane four days later. As soon as I opened the bike box to check things, I found that my tools and one pedal were missing. I had only a week before my departure for Hawaii and needed to feel the bike under me again. I was not up to pedaling with just one leg for 112 miles during the Hawaiian Ironman, so I put on pedals from another bike. I was able to replace the tools, but I couldn't replace the pedal. It was an old model and I knew no one in town would have it, so I called the Speedplay manufacturers directly. They said they'd mail me one immediately. It arrived the day before I left and it was *gratis*, as the original pair had been.

My training time for Hawaii this year had, in fact, been eaten up by travel. I was hoping that the stress of all the logistical challenges would substitute for the stress of training. Would I be able to hold out to the finish in the Hawaiian Ironman this time? I wondered. Shortly before I left for Kona I opened a book with quotes from Thomas Merton that I hadn't looked at for a long time. As I leafed through it I found these words, which seemed to express the essence of my present being: "A true encounter with

Christ liberates something in us, a power we did not know we had, a hope, a capacity for life, a resilience, an ability to bounce back when we thought we were completely defeated, a capacity to grow and change, a power of creative transformation."

I thought, "That really says it!" At least that's what my life seems to have been all about—the ups and downs and pushing through seeming defeats so that they weren't defeats but only opportunities to grow and be strengthened.

As I headed for Hawaii there was a possibility of a tsunami due to an earthquake out in the ocean. "Oh, well," I thought. Life is one big adventure. When I set out to drive from Spokane to Seattle to catch my flight, traffic came to a complete halt on Highway 90 just 60 miles from home. The cause? A dust storm! "Not another one, Lord. Am I being jinxed? I just experienced one a month ago in Australia when the Sydney airport was closed. And now this?"

As traffic was being redirected, I chose the less traveled detour. Dust was blowing so badly, it was all I could do to keep the wheels steady and stare a few yards ahead of me so as not to rear-end any other vehicle. By taking a frontage road and a few detours and driving slowly, I got through. Before leaving Spokane, I had been cautioned by that interior voice to leave two hours earlier than usual—"just in case." Was I ever glad I had listened! Amazingly enough, I got to Seattle at the intended time to enjoy a layover with friends that night.

Early the very next morning I parked my car and jumped on a shuttle to the airport, only to be told my flight had been delayed until midnight. Another angel in the form of the curb attendant, who was watching my bike until I had deposited the car, found me another flight that left only an hour and a half later. Another blessing in disguise! I found myself on the same flight as my friend Cindy Rach, who was also headed for the race in Kona.

Cindy and I made plans to do a practice swim in the ocean the following day. It was just four days before the race, and we both managed to swim the full distance of the course together. This was her first Hawaiian Ironman, and she was very relieved to have done the entire swim. The following day we took our bikes for the challenging fourteen-mile climb to Hawi, the turn-around point on the cycling course.

During the actual race, quite by chance, we actually swam the last quarter mile side by side. When I exited the water a second ahead of her, she yelled, "Thank you, Sister, you were my guiding light." In the changing tent, three volunteers descended on me, which interfered with my focus, as I am used to doing everything myself.

I was about two miles out on the bike when I realized I had no sunglasses. There was no way to turn back now, even though I knew it was going to be a struggle without my glasses. It was hot and windy and I had to guard my eyes the best I could. I did not realize how much this sapped my energy. The glare of the sun beating off the pavement made it seem even hotter.

When I got to the turnaround in Hawi, I was extremely thirsty and aware of being depleted. At the aid station where I had expected to get some water, they had run out. By now I was really feeling weak. I knew I needed some kind of nourishment, but my stomach was not really grateful for anything I put in it. When I reached an aid station that had some water, I couldn't even drink it, so the helpers doused me instead—through my helmet, over my arms, down my front, along my thighs, legs, and some even seeped into my bike shoes.

At first, the water, although not really cold, was a shock. I figured I'd absorb the moisture through my skin and I set out again, but try as I might, I could not get clipped into my left pedal. I had to ride the last twenty-five miles without being secured in my pedal on the left side. Perhaps the water that slipped into the shoe had interfered. This meant I couldn't exert much force on that foot and I couldn't stand up on the pedals to power the hills when needed.

I was just about two miles from bringing the bike into transition when the media on a motorcycle pulled up in front of me with cameras. I was wondering, "Why do they want to shoot me now? I am almost at the tail end." Then Rudy Garcia-Tolson, the double, above-the-knee amputee, whom they had been profiling, came alongside me. "Oh, so this is why the cameras are here," I realized.

Rudy and I were riding side by side. So as not to be caught for drafting, I dropped back temporarily. At the same time, I had a gut feeling that I was racing against time. I waited for my opportunity to surge between Rudy and the media. After I did, I kept waiting for him to repass, but he never did. I thought there might still be a chance for me to make it. Reluctantly, the volunteer who caught my bike when I rolled into transition said, "I am sorry. I am so sorry, you have missed the bike cutoff by a few minutes."

This was the second time in two years this had happened. But again, I thought, "Father knows best." There was no way my body could have gone out on the run and made it to the finish. I was absolutely drained of energy. I had seen other cyclists being picked up and hauled in, so I was grateful to have finished at least two-thirds of this Ironman. I had given it all I had; there was nothing left!

The night before the race, as I lay awake, I amused myself by thinking about the relativity of time and space, and this haiku came to mind:

What are time and space?
Never mind, keep up the pace.
Just finish the race.

Well, maybe next time I will!

When I got back to Seattle, my travel traumas were far from over! My car was missing from the parking slot of the condo complex where I had left it. "Lord, I have trusted you through all my dilemmas, and I am going to trust you now," I prayed, "but please send help soon. I can't wander around here all night long. It is cold, dark, and damp. I'm not in Hawaii any more." Shortly after I had made the rounds of the complex a police car drove in. I flagged it down and explained my situation to the policewoman. It turned out that I had parked my car near a dumpster, thinking that was an unused slot. After the policewoman succeeded in locating the tow company, she drove me there. The owner said I had come just in the nick of time to reclaim the car. It had been towed the afternoon I left, so it was now eight days later, and they were ready to put the car up for auction. In fact, the papers had already been signed.

This was costing me more than the car was worth, but I was glad to have my trusty transportation back. I had named my car Teal Tessie, after "the Little Flower," Saint Thérèse of Lisieux, who is known to pack a lot of influence with the Lord. I am sure she saved my car from the auction block. That night I got to my friend's house after midnight, parked my car in front, and awoke early the next morning. To my dismay it was missing again! My friend and I were stunned! Her first thought was that it had been stolen. I suggested we call the tow company first. Fortunately, I had memorized the number from the night before. It turned out I had parked on an arterial road that was quiet at night, but busily trafficked during the day. I finally got back to Spokane thinking I had had enough travel trauma in a single month to last me my remaining life.

Now the last event for 2009 was in Clearwater, Florida, which was still experiencing the whiplash of Hurricane Ida's tail when I arrived two days early for the 70.3 Ironman World Championship on November 13, several weeks after the Hawaiian Ironman. The ocean was badly ruffled. The red flag was flying. The high winds and agitated surf were a concern for the Race Directors. Those athletes who had come early to train were being battered by the high surf and current. The day before the race, the Race Director made a decision to switch the swim to the harbor side where private boats were moored. This meant that no one had the opportunity, not even the Pros, for a pre-race swim. On race day, the ocean was as placid as it could be. I could just hear the Lord laughing at us, saying, "Oh ye, of little faith."

I hadn't been able to inflate my sew-up tires adequately because of a valve problem, so I knew my bike time would suffer as a consequence. I just prayed, "Lord, you take care of it from here. There's nothing more I can do." My pre-race adventures weren't over yet.

The night before the race, I slashed my right thumb with a pair of folding scissors. I was alone and had nothing in the vacant house where I was staying except toilet tissue. It took practically the whole roll to stop the bleeding. Bandaged up, I finished the entire race seconds short of seven hours just pleased to have made it all the way under the circumstances.

The end of the 2009 race season had come. I was more than ready for it to end! Almost every event had been a struggle. Looking back, I realized my only consistent activity had been swimming indoors. It occurred to me that this much I could keep doing through my 90s.

22

Fight Against Time

Sometimes you best your competition simply by outliving them!

MY MOTHER USED to say, "Why don't you act your age?" Now I am glad I never adhered to that cautionary advice. I'd rather remain still a child at heart. After all, when reaching eighty, who would want to act her age? I don't notice myself getting old because my spirit isn't there just yet. Sometimes, when I see older people, I am a little curious about their age compared to mine. So many people seem to be struggling with their poor little bodies long before I am. It makes me almost feel guilty to be on the go as I am. On the other hand, I feel very blessed and very grateful so keep on going as if there were no time limits. I think it's best not to pay any attention to age, but to who you are while you are in the process of getting there.

When it comes to training, aging up requires a shift in strategy. When you get to be as old as I am, you don't have to go out and do hard-core training like the younger set. If I am just consistent and keep my body moving, I am less susceptible to fatigue and injury unless I encounter the unforeseen, such as landing on the asphalt unintentionally! In these instances, I still seem to have quick recovery time and get back on track long before the doctors' predictions. On the other hand, it is a physical feat just to get out of bed in the morning sometimes. It's my daily jog to Mass that catapults me.

I chuckled when I ran across this quote: "Age is a matter of mind. If you don't mind, it doesn't either." These words express just how I view aging. It is really better not even to refer to it—except of course in competition when you want to know who to beat! This way, it just creeps up on you without you even realizing it.

I have tried to respect my age and not push beyond reason. That is when accidents are most likely to happen, and it is easy to become disheartened. The spirit can be knocked out of kilter as well as the body. I have spent my life attempting to squeeze as much as I can into twenty-four hours. But now when I have a few lethargic days, I respect them and let it be. It's okay to back off so as to avoid going down. It takes prudence to know when to push and when to hold back.

Oddly enough, my best records have been when I've had only moderate training during the season. I suppose the reality is that I am conserving energy for the race and am more eager to go when the event rolls around. For the more mature athlete, I think endurance is the key, not necessarily speed. If you can endure, you can outdo the speedsters who wear themselves out in the beginning stages. The passing years have taken some speed out of me. The older I get, the slower I get, but usually I get there.

Looking back, I think I began peaking around my seventh year of running, before I ever attempted a triathlon. I had been competing in about twenty runs annually. One year I had even done seven marathons, but I paid the price. I knew I was burned out when I didn't even want to look at a pair of running shoes. I'm not sure I have ever experienced a runner's high, but I have surely felt the lows. God's intervention cured that. Being introduced to triathlons was my salvation.

By the close of 2009, I had done more than 340 triathlons, including 45 Ironman events. The numbers are still adding up because I am still competing. By now I have gotten used to being not only the oldest woman, but the oldest participant in practically every triathlon I engage in. At first that realization came as a shock. Since pioneering the 75–79 age group for women in the Canadian Ironman, I haven't had any competition in that age group for this distance. Now that I'm preparing to open an 80-plus spot for women, I hope my former group won't be left vacant for too much longer.

No matter what I do it seems like I am always racing against time. It is getting more and more difficult to reach the finish line in seventeen hours. I sabotage an otherwise good swim and good bike when I can't run because my stomach won't cooperate, something that's been happening for more than ten years. Now when I do finish an Ironman distance, it's by a slim margin. I used to set age-group records. Now the only way I can do that is by outliving the competition.

How can I explain the desire to keep going? At one point when I had reached sixty I thought I was going to give up this foolishness. Well, then, maybe seventy. Now that I am eighty, I no longer entertain the idea of quitting unless my battery runs low. It has been more than thirty-one years since I first put on a pair of running shoes, and people keep telling me, "Oh you are such an inspiration. We love to see you here. Please don't stop." Then I say, "O, Lord, if you want me to be a mascot for these athletes, keep feeding me the energy so as not to disappoint them. I'm relying on you to let me know when to stop." If it were up to me, I would have done it yesterday!

My long-lasting records have been broken. I just can't understand why it took so long. There were people out there capable of doing it, but perhaps they just didn't realize it. When I was up on the platform in my fifties I would be the only woman. I even remember saying, when receiving my award at the Capitol City Marathon in Olympia, Washington, "I'm lonely up here. When is someone going to join me?" After I merged into triathlons I was still without much company in the 55–59 age group, and held that age group record in the Canadian Ironman for close to fifteen years. Finally, when I reached my sixties, triathlons had caught on and women were becoming eager to *tri*.

Currently the 65–69 age group is well populated. It has made me happy to see these age groups expanding. Even though "the old gray mare ain't what she used to be," I still enjoy the camaraderie. I have met friends of all ages through the course of years. They keep me going. They are *my* heroes.

At the age of seventy-eight, during the 2008 Moses Lake Triathlon in my home state of Washington, I was coming out of transition on my bike when someone in her forties yelled at me, "I want to be just like you when I grow up!" This is not the first time I have heard this, but it is the first time I remember responding. "Don't ever grow up!" I could hear laughter in the background, but what I didn't have time to add was, "Never lose sight of your child. It is the purest, most unadulterated authentic part of you."

On the run portion of this same triathlon, just before getting to the turnaround, I saw a person lying on his back right in the middle of the course. Shortly before I got to the spot, the person struggled to stand up. As I was drawing closer, I could see he was a middle-aged man. As I passed him I yelled out, "You're going to make it to the finish!" He had a rather dazed look on his face, so I was not exactly sure whether my words of encouragement would be fulfilled or not. However, my passing him with age "78" visible on my right leg seemed to have been enough to spur him onward. The result? He crossed the finish line just in front of me.

During the 2002 Hawaiian Ironman, while I was walking a portion of the marathon in the dark under the full moon, I was remembering how much I admired my father, who had been a champion oarsman and had played the vigorous game of handball until he was seventy. It brought back memories of how he and I portaged his canoe down the steep slopes to the Merrimac River for our last canoe trip together, celebrating his seventieth birthday. He was at the stern, still issuing commands as usual. While I was reflecting on this, it dawned on me, "Hey, you are already two years beyond seventy doing this Ironman thing." It made me wonder if my father could ever have done this. I could almost hear him bellow an emphatic, "No, nor would I want to cover 140.6 miles without a motor or a paddle!"

Then and only then did I realize, Hey, maybe what you are doing *is* a little unusual. Until then I hadn't given it a second thought. With this in mind I picked up the pace, projecting to the finish in 16:48:04 hours, winning my age group 70–74 title again. A rather extensive day!

As the saying goes, "Records are made to be broken," but now I have none to break unless it be my own. As it unfolded it took thirteen and eleven years respectively for my two Hawaiian Ironman records for women 60–64 and women 65–69 to be broken in 2005. So, I opened a new age group for women 75–79 at the same time. If I happen to open a new one for women age 80-plus this coming year, I may have to come back when I'm 90 and do it all over again in order to fulfill Jim Ward's prophecy: "If anyone can do these [Ironman] distances in their 90s, it will be Sister Madonna." I don't know where he got that idea, but I hope he's right.

The year 2010 would be the twenty-fifth since my first Hawaiian Ironman and a milestone for me in many ways. I'd like to open up the eighty-plus age group for women in both the Hawaiian and Canadian Ironman events, although there are times when I wonder how I can keep primed for this. When the doubt creeps in and I long for a softer lifestyle, I pray, "Lord, if this is what you want, I will keep going until you put me out of commission." Of course, He nearly did during the 2000 Hawaiian Ironman. After that crash, some wondered if I would ever return. Each year since, I have reentered Kona to do my best, no matter the circumstances. Each time, I have wondered if this would be my last race, but I have always come back so far. If I succeed in this goal of opening a new age group for women, I may take a vacation from the Ironman distances and concentrate on shorter distances with the Half Ironman being max.

It is my faith that has carried me through life's ups and downs. Whenever injured, I wait for the Lord to pick me up again and set me on my feet, confidently reminding Him, "God, you know, my intent is to keep running toward you." How long will I persevere in doing these triathlons? Only God knows, and I want to listen. This I do know: "The life and death of each of us has its influence on others. If we live, we live for the Lord; if we die, we die for the Lord; so whether we live or die, we belong to the Lord." (Romans 14:7–8) A consoling thought for us all. I realize that it is the intention with which you do anything, anything at all, that makes it of value in the eyes of the Lord. Because of my intention more than thirty years ago to help salvage a loved one, I have been given the grace to race.

I have fought the good fight,
I have finished the race,
I have kept the faith.
      —2 Timothy 4:7.

Afterword

I'M NOT QUITE sure what first prompted me to begin an autobiography, but after I started running and then competing, I was approached periodically by the media. When I committed myself to competing in the Boston Marathon in 1982 for multiple sclerosis, for instance, the story was picked up by the Associated Press. In subsequent years, articles appeared in numerous magazines and newspapers and there was TV coverage as well. Perhaps it occurred to me to give the whole story once and for all. I titled my early account *Miracles and Marathons*. But then I began doing triathlons, and the manuscript sat on the back burner. Although I was piling up more material all the time, there was simply no time left to write about my experiences, so I abandoned the cause.

Several years ago, literary agent Elisabeth Weed happened to watch my profile on HBO *Real Sports* with Bryant Gumble (first aired on February 11, 2007). She approached the producer, saying, "This story has got to be put into print." When Tim Walker, the HBO producer, alerted me to her idea, I balked. I figured I was still too busy living life to write about it. It was also hard for me to understand how my little old life could be of interest to anyone.

I was urged gradually to sacrifice my hold on time, if indeed there was an interest. While laboring over this book I became increasingly aware that a life lived in earnest is not for oneself. I also considered I owed it to my triathlon community that has always been so supportive. Since this undertaking was not of my own volition, I came to understand that if this was of Divine compulsion, I should cooperate. I thought of Thérèse of Lisieux, a young Carmelite nun, who was asked by her Superior, who also happened to be her blood sister, to write her autobiography. She too was reluctant but did so because of her vow of obedience. Therefore, I invited Saint Thérèse, popularly known as "the Little Flower," to be the patroness of my arduous undertaking, hoping that what emerges will be of benefit to whoever thumbs the pages of this autobiography as well the random reflections that follow. Now that this is all said and done, I stand back to gain perspective and marvel at how our individual contacts are so delicately interwoven in the fabric of life. To me life will forever remain a mystery, not something to be exploited or taken for granted. All has been given and meant to be returned to the Giver. From Creator to receiver to returner constitutes a sacred cycle, a Blessed Trinity.

It is my hope that you, the reader, will garner something from the bits and pieces of this prolonged life that will resonate with your own. I invite you to explore your own depths and come to appreciate who you are and, thus, what you can do.

Reflections

You can soar if you feel like it!

A WORD TO the hesitant: Anyone can run. If you can walk, you can run. It takes no more skill than that. It comes as naturally as breathing. A lot of people are their own worst enemies. When they start thinking about their age, they say, "Oh, this hurts, that hurts, I can't do this, I can't do that."

Well, so what? When you were a kid, you didn't bother about what hurt, you just went out and did it. It is beautiful to watch children running with sheer abandonment. They do it more often than walking. The next step is to recall that you were once a child. Picture yourself running like they do, then do it!

So what if you tip the scales at two hundred pounds? Your legs have carried you this far, and they can carry you a lot farther a lot quicker with running steps. Turn on the motor of your mind and willpower and go for it.

Gear up your determination. It will help to set a goal, have a personal impetus for getting motivated if for no other reason than being practical. Think of all the gas you can save by literally running errands to department stores, post offices, and grocery stores (as long as you are not carrying eggs). Give yourself a reason to get out there. Then challenge your friends to enter a race with you. It's a great feeling when you cross that finish line.

Start now. Don't let your age be an obstacle. Remember: It's never too late to start. Thus we never get too old to experience something new. Be patient. Your body is a very faithful instrument and will respond to your commands.

Begin gradually. Each day, each week, set a little goal for yourself, and then increase the margin. Your body needs to get acquainted with that kind of anaerobic and aerobic exercise. Once you get synchronized, there is no end to what you can do. Just be reasonable in your expectations. What might be good for one might not be good for another. So respect yourself for your own capabilities. In other words, race within yourself—not against someone else.

A note of caution: You've got a three-wheel drive: body, mind, and soul. The power is there to use, not to overuse or abuse. If you let your goal become your master, you are in danger of being enslaved by the very process you feel gives you freedom. This is true of any addiction. So take heed, lest you lose the freedom to decide how many miles *you* want to do in a day. Rather listen to what your body is suggesting.

To the compulsive: There's more to life than running. You can't afford to cheat yourself of the spontaneous surprises the day may offer just because you think you have to put in a certain number of miles. A running acquaintance of mine once shared that he used to wonder if it was the lonely who ran, or whether running made for loneliness. It can be either way or neither.

If you do not have the support of those you live with, it becomes a meaningless venture that contributes to loneliness. The time devoted to running instead of being with family could stir up some resentment unless you establish balance.

Running can also be a cop-out for not doing other things. It can absorb your whole attention, causing you to neglect yourself and the other dimensions in your life. Take a day or two off from running during the week. Your body and mind deserve the vacation. Then you can remain fresh and running won't run you!

Let each day surprise you. We are here to learn. Every day holds in store a new experience and a new beginning. Take life as it comes, enjoy what you can, and tolerate the rest. Take time to be alone in nature. It lifts the soul.

Develop your faith. I have never been in total panic. No matter what the circumstance, I know there will always be help. Trust and it will happen. It's a deep knowing inside that God is not going to let me down. The more one practices faith, the more it grows. I love this quote: "We can rejoice too when we run into problems and trials for we know that they are good for us—they help us learn to be patient. Patience develops strength of character in us and helps us trust God more each time we use it until finally our hope and faith are strong and steady. When this happens, we are ready to hold our heads high no matter what happens and know that all is well, for we know how clearly God loves us." (Romans 5:3–5).

Use your talents. Every now and then a line from Antoine de Saint-Exupéry's *The Little Prince*, which was required reading in college, comes to mind. Paraphrased it runs something like this: "Once you have discovered a gift it is your responsibility to use it." If we aren't grateful for the gifts God has given us, we snub

Him. We cannot control inspiration. It flows through us from our higher source, so we must remain open channels and let his grace flow through us.

Be grateful. Whenever anything adverse happens, I tend to count my blessings. Sometimes I could curse, but that isn't healing and makes no sense. Instead, I center on being totally grateful just to be alive to tell the tale and carry on.

Take time to be still. To listen with distraction is to remain empty. To listen with inner stillness is to be filled with peace and wisdom.

Concentrate on people, not things. Despite the indulgence of numerous sponsors for which I have always been grateful, my thrust is to live a simple life, rejecting suggestions from friends to get a computer, cell phone, BlackBerry, blueberry, blog, iPod, etc. I have learned the hard way that *the less you have the less you have to worry about.*

On two occasions my bike was stolen, throwing me into a tizzy. During travel, two bags were ripped off, one containing my competition paraphernalia and the other a camera which I had intended to use during my touring. After spending a week mourning my violation, I realized that you can do without things, and cover your losses but not without the people who befriend you. In essence, *life is all about relationships, not material objects.* In other words, a person who has nothing can't be ripped off!

Honor the smallest steps. Sometimes I wonder how little old me in my semisequestered state can make any difference to anyone. Then I am reminded how pennies multiply in a jar. I also recollect how a mile is added to a marathon, step by step, and how hours are created in a day, minute by minute. Then I recalled how I tackled a downed tree that had fallen partially onto the house of an aged neighbor, who was hospitalized at the time, during our 1996 ice storm in Spokane. It looked like an overwhelming task until I resolved to dismember it branch by branch. So it is that blessings of self are distributed through such small acts of kindness.

With this in mind, it is obvious that even the most insignificant action adds to the grand scheme of life. Everyone was made for a unique purpose. When grappling with our purpose in life, it helps to realize that perhaps *the journey itself is actually the purpose*, so let's watch our step!

Watch for your angels. You never know what form your angels are going to take. Sometimes they appear and show you the way. They can appear when least expected, and depart just as quickly. You never know what they'll look like. They are simply there when you need them. "Do not forget to entertain strangers, for by so doing some have unwittingly entertained angels." (Hebrews 13:2). You may actually be one of these angels for another!

Acknowledgments

For all those persons woven into the fabric of my life, I feel extremely blessed, and I thank them from the depths of my being. There is no need to mention names. They know who they are. Even though miles may separate us, I'll always remember these spirit-filled relationships and the people who have added such joy to my life through their encouragement, enthusiasm, and loving support. Should we meet again tomorrow, I am certain we would simply take up where we left off. Thank you all for being there for me. To accept and be accepted, to love and be loved, is the Grand Finale of Life.

I am also grateful to the many race directors who have allowed me to do their events without exacting an entry fee and to the many persons who have shared their homes as my home away from home. Without these acts of kindness I would not have appeared on the triathlon scene nearly as frequently as I have.

I would also like to recognize those sponsors whose products and apparel have taken me through these thirty years of competition. They are listed according to the order of items received:

New Balance for shoes

Nike for shoes

Centurion for Dave Scott First Signature Tri bike

Profile for add-on bars

Suburban Machinery for Litespeed bike

Zipp for race wheels

Sparrow for add-on bars

Clif Bars for nutrition

Speedplay for pedals

Carnac for bike shoes

Calfee for Tri bike

Brooks for running shoes and apparel

Cannondale for bike and appointments

Hed for race wheels

Newton for running shoes

Zoot for shoes and apparel

K-Swiss for shoes